THE
BIRTH
OF A
HYMN

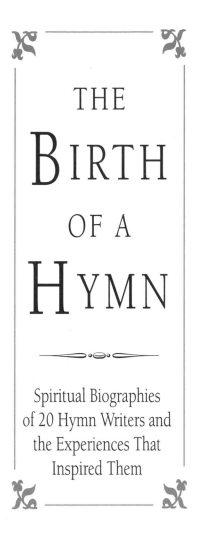

THE
BIRTH
OF A
HYMN

Spiritual Biographies
of 20 Hymn Writers and
the Experiences That
Inspired Them

BY KEITH SCHWANZ

PUBLISHING
COMPANY

KANSAS CITY, MO 64141

Dedication

I was four years old when I sang my first solo in church. In 1958 the Church of the Nazarene in Grand Island, Nebraska, held children's church in the basement. We turned off the lights in the windowless room and I held a candle as I sang, "I'm a little candle shining in the dark." I remember standing near the piano so the pianist could see the music. I dedicate this book to the woman who was my accompanist that day, my mother, Myrtle Schwanz.

CONTENTS

About the Author

Nothing energizes Dr. Keith Schwanz like the synthesis of good biblical exegesis, clear doctrinal exposition, fervent spiritual experience, and beautiful artistic expression in a hymn text. He has spent his life preparing to contribute to an interdisciplinary understanding of church music. Dr. Schwanz has training in both religious studies and musical studies.

Dr. Schwanz is an ordained elder in the Church of the Nazarene and currently is the pastor of the Columbia Ridge Church of the Nazarene in Portland, Oregon. In addition to his pastoral duties, he has written articles for several publications and lectured on church music topics at seminaries, colleges, and conferences. He is a member of the Wesleyan Theological Society and the Hymn Society in the United States and Canada. Dr. Schwanz served on the Advisory Committee for the *Sing to the Lord* hymnal and prepared *Resources for Worship Planning*, a companion to the hymnal.

His wife, Judi, is also an ordained minister in the Church of the Nazarene and is the director of the Graduate Department of Counseling at Western Evangelical Seminary. They have two college-aged children, Karla and Jason.

Foreword

The songs we sing are more satisfying to us emotionally, and also more potent as aids to worship, if we associate them with personal roots, such as a mother's voice, or the church of our childhood. Even more moving is a song whose author is a friend, and whose reason for writing the song is a personal treasure to us.

Second best to knowing the author personally is "meeting" him or her through the printed page. When we associate a poignant story, this greatly increases the song's power to bless our hearts. As we sing the song, we feel the warmth of the grace that produced the song, and we enter into that grace.

This is the special ministry of the following stories. Dr. Keith Schwanz has carefully researched not only the spiritual biographies of the authors of these best-loved songs but especially the real-life crises that prompted their writing.

And no one is better qualified to enrich our worship this way than Dr. Schwanz. Though a pastor and a strong preacher, he is a specialist in church music. This claim is supported not just by his Ph.D. earned in church music but by his years of experience as a music minister and worship leader. He has a rare ability to weave song, word, and action into a harmonious tapestry of corporate worship.

Dr. Schwanz is making a lasting contribution to the Holiness Movement by providing this fascinating glimpse of the spiritual lives of the men and women behind our contemporary Wesleyan hymnody.

—Richard S. Taylor

Acknowledgments

I gratefully acknowledge the assistance of many people as I prepared this book. Their contributions made my research more complete. Thanks to:

Stan Ingersol and the staff of the Church of the Nazarene Archives

Donna Watson of the Wesleyan Church Archives

the library staff of the Western Evangelical Seminary

Linda Doezema of the Houghton College Library

Floyd and Ruth Hawkins, Byron Carmony, Otis Skillings, Steve Adams, and Ken Bible for granting me interviews

Bernice Dietrich for the information on her mother, Lorene Good

Catherine Fehr and Richard Gerig, sister and friend of David Ives

Ken Bible, David McDonald, and Joyce Shank of Lillenas Publishing Company

and many others who provided tidbits of information and words of encouragement

Finally, I'm grateful for the church board and people of the Portland, Oregon, Columbia Ridge Church of the Nazarene who urged their pastor to tell another hymn story. Most of all, thanks to my wife, Judi, who is not only my best editor but also my constant encourager.

Introduction

In the Bible's hymnbook we often find the psalmist David writing from his experiences. The events in his life generated hymnic expressions. David wrote Ps. 3 after he fled from his son, Absalom. In this psalm David talked about the enemies who pursued him and the protection God provided. Ps. 30 was written for the dedication of the Temple, and David filled it with praise for God's faithfulness. David praised the Lord for answered prayer in Ps. 34 after he feigned insanity before Abimelech. Ps. 51 expressed David's cry for God's mercy and cleansing after the prophet Nathan confronted him about his adultery with Bathsheba. When Saul sent a surveillance team to stalk David, David sang of the strength of the Lord in Ps. 59. While David was in the desert of Judah, he wrote of his desire for God in Ps. 63, "My soul thirsts for you" (v. 1b).

Likewise, many of the hymns and songs that comprise the church's repertoire were born in the spiritual experiences of their authors. God lifted them out of the slimy pit of sin and gave them firm footing on Christ the Solid Rock. The joy of this experience erupted in "a new song . . . a hymn of praise to our God" (Ps. 40:3). The spiritual experience preluded the hymn writing.

In this book I introduce some writers who gave us the songs we love to sing. My main objective is to provide glimpses of the hymn writers' spiritual journeys and, where possible, to make a connection between their spiritual experiences and their hymnic expressions.

This is a book of spiritual biographies. Fanny Crosby wrote, "Redeemed, how I love to proclaim it!" In this book I explore the connection between redemption and proclamation, spiritual experience and poetic expression in the lives of hymn writers. Where possible I have let the person testify with his or her own words; some quotes are lengthy for that reason.

Some of the hymn writers featured in this book were pastors. Others were evangelists or city mission workers. Still others were faithful laypersons. However, they all were touched by God and sought to express themselves in a way that would show others the source of their inspiration.

I considered three groups of readers as I wrote this book. The first group includes all Christians. I have prayed that many people will find helpful devotional material in this book. I hope your spirit is encouraged as you read about the pilgrimages of other Christians. Their examples are often inspiring. Knowing a little about the person behind the hymn often helps worshipers see new nuances in the hymn text. I desire for you to be spiritually strengthened as you read this book.

The second group for whom I've written are the pastors and church musicians who lead worship. Beyond the devotional value, this volume can be used as a ministry tool. Preachers will find sermon illustrations in these stories. Choir directors might use parts of this book for devotions during choir rehearsals. Worship leaders can use selected elements of these stories to introduce congregational songs. A drama team director might use information from this book to create a vignette for actors and/or readers. This book contains a great deal of information and is a reference tool for the worship leader.

The third part of my intended audience is those who study hymnody. While many books of hymn stories include a broad spectrum of hymn writers, I have been highly selective. The writers profiled in this book are somehow connected to the American Holiness Movement.

Many of the hymn writers in the 19th-century Wesleyan/Holiness Movement were members of the Methodist Episcopal Church. As the movement progressed and denominations were formed around Wesleyan/Holiness distinctives—such as the Church of the Nazarene, the Church of God (Anderson), and The Wesleyan Church—the work of other hymn writers emerged. This book is the first account of some hymn writers' lives and work. Other writers are more widely known, but their connection with the Wesleyan/Holiness Movement may not be realized.

In 1923, Edmund Lorenz wrote *Church Music* in which he identified "a movement entirely independent of that of Bradbury, Lowry, and Doane, which . . . grew out of the more devout side of the 'Spiritual' among the Methodists of Pennsylvania and New Jersey, and had its center at Philadelphia and Ocean Grove, where a great camp-meeting was and is annually held."[1] The focus of this volume is to highlight some of the hymn writers who created and continued this movement.

John Wesley, the patriarch of the Wesleyan/Holiness Movement, wrote seven "Rules for Singing" in an attempt to improve the congregational singing of his day. His final rule stated, "Above all sing spiritually. Have an eye to God in every word you sing. Aim at pleasing Him more than yourself, or any other creature. In order to do this attend strictly to the sense of what you sing, and see that your heart is not carried away with the sound, but offered to God continually; so shall your singing be such as the Lord will approve here, and reward you when He cometh in the clouds of heaven." Wesley had a high view of congregational singing. He believed that through the hymns of the church spiritual formation would occur. As a spiritual descendent of John Wesley, I hope this book enriches your hymn singing and your spiritual life as you "grow in the grace and knowledge of our Lord and Savior Jesus Christ" (2 Pet. 3:18).

Phoebe Palmer
(1807-74)

Phoebe knew the emptiness she felt had a spiritual origin. Her parents had provided a fervent Christian environment for her when she was a child. She could not recall a time in her life when she did not consider herself a disciple of Jesus Christ. When she married Walter Palmer, a physician in New York City, they immediately established a home centered on Christ. Phoebe was encouraged by her husband's involvement in the ministry of the Allen Street Methodist Episcopal Church. His spiritual fervor warmed her soul, but the ember soon sputtered and cooled. In her diary on April 28, 1832, Phoebe wrote, "I am getting along feebly in the divine life, not so much lacking in good purposes as in carrying out my ever earnest resolve."[2]

Phoebe wondered if her devotion to her children blocked her relationship with God. Two sons died in infancy. Sarah, a daughter born in April 1833, was strong and healthy. Eliza, born in August 1835, was not. Phoebe herself was not well. As both she and her daughter lay near death, Phoebe asked God to spare their lives. She asked for further opportunities to live a godly life, pledging to serve the Lord by writing religious poetry and by other means.[3]

Both of the females' health improved, but tragedy lay ahead. One summer evening Phoebe laid Eliza in her cradle. A friend was visiting, so Phoebe left Eliza in the care of a nursemaid. An alcohol lamp needed to be filled, which the maid started to do without blowing out the wick. The lamp burst into flames, burning the maid's hands. With a reflexive motion, she threw the lamp away from her. The lamp landed in Eliza's crib, spreading fuel and flames. Eliza lived only a few hours.

In despair, Phoebe shut herself into a room. She paced the floor. She cried. She begged God to answer her shouts of "Why?" Then Phoebe opened her Bible and read, "O the depth of the riches both of the wisdom and knowledge of God! how unsearchable are his judgments, and his ways past finding out!" (Rom. 11:33, KJV). "That moment began a mystical experience that shaped the rest of her life.

. . . In the midst of her pain and anger, she felt God telling her to stop blaming the freakish circumstances for her daughter's death, to stop blaming herself for employing such a careless nurse, and to stop blaming the nurse for her horrible stupidity. . . . Phoebe stopped crying and made a conscious choice to trust God's goodness and love."[4]

Phoebe's spiritual journey started gaining momentum that day but did not reach full speed for another two years. In her diary on July 27, 1837, Phoebe wrote about her experience the previous day, "Between the hours of eight and nine o'clock yesterday I was led by the Spirit to the determination that I would never rest, day nor night, until I knew that the spring of every motive was pure and that the consecration I made of myself was wholly accepted."[5]

A spiritual battle ensued. As Phoebe sought to make a total consecration, the tempter questioned her about her intentions. She did not let the satanic inquiry distract her until eventually "the enemy had no further ground for questioning, relative to the consecration, whether it was entire, absolute and unconditional. From the depths of my being I felt that the consecration was absolute."[6]

The tempter attacked from another direction, suggesting that God would not receive her. Phoebe countered with the promises of the Bible that assured her that God welcomes the person who comes by faith. Phoebe wrote in her diary: "I had thought of the doctrine of faith as difficult. Now I saw that it was only to believe heartily what in fact I had always professed to believe—that is, that the Bible is the word of God just as truly as though I could hear Him speaking in tones of thunder from Sinai's Mount, and faith is to believe it!"[7]

Phoebe continued:

> Yet, though I knew that it could not be otherwise than that God did receive me, my faith was at once put to the test. I had expected that some wonderful manifestation would at once follow as the reward of my faith. But I was shut up to faith—naked faith in a naked promise.
>
> The next step, faith, in regard to divine acceptance of all, had also been distinctly taken. And now, as I plainly saw the third step clearly defined in the word, I took the advanced ground—confession.
>
> Giving God the glory due to His name, I exclaimed, "Through Thy grace alone I have been enabled to give myself wholly and forever to Thee. Thou hast given Thy word, assuring me that Thou dost receive. I believe that word! Alleluia! the

Lord God Omnipotent reigneth unrivaled in my heart. Glory be to the Father! Glory be to the Son! Glory be to the Holy Spirit forever!" O, into what a region of light, glory and purity, was my soul at this moment ushered! I felt that I was but a drop in the ocean of infinite love, and Christ was all in all.[8]

From that day, July 26, 1837, Phoebe Palmer began a ministry that fanned into flame the 19th-century Holiness revivals. By 1840 Phoebe led the Tuesday Meeting for the Promotion of Holiness. These meetings were started by her sister, Sarah Lankford, and were first held in the house shared by the Palmers and the Lankfords. The meetings followed a simple order: scripture reading, hymn, prayer, testimonies of sanctification, and exhortations about Holiness.

> *Amazing grace!*
> *'tis heav'n below*
> *To feel the blood applied,*
> *And Jesus, only Jesus know,*
> *My Jesus, crucified.*

At first only women attended. Four years later men were invited. The meetings became so popular that eventually as many as 300 people crowded into the Palmer house. Phoebe Palmer's Tuesday Meeting became a model for the Tuesday Afternoon Holiness Meeting used by many holiness groups, including the first congregation known as the Church of the Nazarene.[9]

In 1842 Phoebe wrote and published *The Way of Holiness*, a book that eventually sold 100,000 copies worldwide. By 1850 Walter and Phoebe Palmer had begun preaching tours. From 1859 to 1863 they traveled extensively in Europe, preaching the Holiness message wherever they went. In 1863 Walter purchased the periodical *Guide to Holiness*. Phoebe acted as the editor until her death.

Phoebe Palmer emerged as a prominent leader of the Wesleyan/Holiness Movement in the 19th century because of the magnitude of her ministry. Her extensive work as a writer and speaker influenced scores of people who continued the work of the Holiness Movement after her death.

"The Cleansing Wave" (*Sing to the Lord* No. 520)

Phoebe Palmer wrote many hymns and poems. In 1831 she wrote an ode for Independence Day, celebrating freedom in the United States, but lamenting the bondage of African slaves. In 1833 she wrote a hymn for her congregation's Sunday School. Phoebe wrote three hymns for the 50th anniversary celebration of American Methodism in 1834. In 1839 she wrote four hymns for the 100th anniversary of worldwide Methodism.[10]

"The Cleansing Wave" was written sometime before 1873. George Hughes, in his report of 14 holiness camp meetings held between 1867 and 1872, described this hymn being sung. "The Cleansing Wave" was "sung with good effect in the forest temple, while precious souls plunge into the cleansing stream, rising renewed in all the life of God."[11]

When compared with the sanctification hymns of Charles Wesley, this hymn illustrates some of the ways Phoebe Palmer augmented the teachings of John and Charles Wesley. For example, in "Jesus, Thine All-victorious Love" (*Sing to the Lord* No. 500), Charles Wesley asked God to send the Refining Fire.

> *O that it now from heav'n might fall,*
>   *And all my sins consume!*
> *Come, Holy Ghost, for Thee I call;*
>   *Spirit of Burning, come!*
> *Refining Fire, go thro' my heart;*
>   *Illuminate my soul.*
> *Scatter Thy life through ev'ry part,*
>   *And sanctify the whole.*

Wesley's hymn is a prayer that God will bring inner purity, a heart of love.

In contrast, Phoebe's hymn celebrates God's completed work. Whereas John Wesley asked his preachers, "Are you going on to perfection?" and in doing so revealed his interest in the sanctification process, Phoebe Palmer emphasized the present possibility of being sanctified wholly. In the refrain of "The Cleansing Wave," Phoebe said:

> *The cleansing stream, I see, I see!*
> *I plunge and, O it cleanseth me!*
> *O praise the Lord, it cleanseth me!*
> *It cleanseth me, yes, cleanseth me!*

In Phoebe's hymn God's work has been completed. The result for Phoebe is not only a clean heart but also a new lifestyle. She stated in stanza 3:

> *I rise to walk in heav'n's own light*
> *Above the world and sin.*

Phoebe's daughter, Phoebe Palmer Knapp, wrote the music for this hymn. Phoebe Palmer Knapp is best known for the tune she wrote for Fanny Crosby's hymn "Blessed Assurance." As far as we know, "The Cleansing Wave" is the only hymn on which mother and daughter collaborated.

Phoebe Palmer had a close friendship with both Mary James and Fanny Crosby. For more information on James, see pages 24-27. For more information on Crosby, see pages 28-37.

FOR FURTHER READING

Raser, Harold E. *Phoebe Palmer: Her Life and Thought.* Lewiston, New York: Mellen Press, 1987.

White, Charles Edward. *The Beauty of Holiness.* Grand Rapids: Francis Asbury Press, 1986.

Mary D. James
(1810-83)

When Mary was invited to be the Sunday School teacher for six little girls who were from six to nine years old, she declined. She felt her young age and lack of knowledge obstructed her chance for success. But the Sunday School superintendent persisted. The pastor and other adults encouraged Mary to reconsider. Finally, because she believed their insistence was an indication of God's will, Mary accepted the position. Mary was only 13.[12]

Mary's class grew until she was responsible for 12 girls. Not content to see her "lambs" only on Sundays, she often invited them to her home. If one was ill, Mary would visit her, often taking a gift. Her contacts with the girls were more than social; she always looked for opportunities to lead them to the Good Shepherd.

The Sunday School superintendent had freely approached Mary about teaching because of the obvious health of Mary's own soul. Mary was just 10 years old when, during a revival meeting, she realized her need for forgiveness. Mary, speaking in the third person, wrote, "The sermon that evening was deeply impressive and powerful; every word seemed as if spoken to her own heart."[13]

When the invitation was given, however, she could not get to the front of the sanctuary because so many people had gathered at the altar. One man, sensing her desire to go forward, carried her through the crowd and placed her at the altar. Mary prayed for some time "without obtaining the desire of her heart."[14] After they went home Mary's mother encouraged her to continue praying about her soul. Three days later, February 18, 1821, Mary was converted at a prayer meeting. Two years later at another prayer meeting, Mary experienced the "all-cleansing blood" and "her heart was made pure."[15] Mary was saved when she was 10, sanctified when she was 12, and active in ministry when she was 13.

For another 60 years Mary proclaimed the good news of full salvation. She spent many years as a Sunday School teacher and superintendent. Her concern for children continued her entire life.

Often she prayed with people who responded to an altar call. "If ever heaven and earth came together, it was when her pleading voice was heard in behalf of a company of contrite ones seeking Jesus."[16] When a service closed without complete victory, Mary would arrange to meet with the person at another time to continue the spiritual quest in private. "Faithfully, yet tenderly, each idol was sought out and held up to the gaze of the hesitating one, until the last was dethroned and the heart completely yielded to Him whose right it is to rule. Patiently, as well as with consummate wisdom, was the Object of faith held up before one whose lack was in this direction, until, like Thomas, the doubting one could say, 'My Lord and my God!'"[17]

Mary became active in the temperance movement. She not only participated in a demonstration before the New Jersey legislature but also helped intoxicated people. On the way home from a camp meeting in 1864, a young man stumbled onto the train in which Mary rode. Since the only vacant seat was next to Mary, she invited him to sit next to her. Throughout the trip to Boston, Mary talked with the young man about his need for salvation. At their destination, she convinced the man to help her carry the camping gear to her home. After he ate dinner with the James family, he slept until the effects of alcohol passed. The next day Mary persuaded him to attend a nearby camp meeting where he was converted.

All for Jesus! all for Jesus!
All my being's ransomed powers:
All my thoughts and words and doings,
All my days and all my hours.
Let my hands perform His bidding;
Let my feet run in His ways;
Let my eyes see Jesus only;
Let my lips speak forth His praise.

Mary participated in many Holiness camp meetings, sometimes attending several in one summer. At the founding of Ocean Grove, New Jersey, a lot was assigned to her on which she had a cabin constructed. She spent several entire summers at Ocean Grove, finding rest for her body and refreshment for her soul. If Walter and Phoebe Palmer could not lead the daily Holiness meeting, Mary would substitute.

Mary's ministry included writing four books and scores of articles for the leading religious periodicals. Many articles from her pen appeared in the *Guide to Holiness*, including a regular column for children. She wrote many poems and more than 50 hymns. About her writing habits, her son and biographer wrote:

> The muse often came to her in wakeful hours of the night. Then, when she rose in the morning, she would first "scribble" and afterward carefully copy the results of her cogitations. An occurrence of special interest, a thought suggested in a discourse, or in something she read, or caught in conversation, would set the active brain at work, and the result would be an article in prose or verse which would soon find its way to one of her editor friends. Rarely were her offerings of this sort declined.[18]

When Mary was born, her mother had named her with Luke 10 in mind, praying "that her little one might choose the good part and ever sit at the feet of Jesus."[19] The name choice was prophetic, for throughout her life Mary lived an exemplary life of adoration for her Savior. Whether teaching a Sunday School class, talking with a seeker, or writing a hymn, Mary sought to lift up the name of Jesus.

"All for Jesus" (*Sing to the Lord* No. 470)

In her New Year's letter for 1871, Mary wrote:

> On reviewing the past year I see much to be thankful for as well as much reason for humiliation. While I wish from my heart that I had done more for Jesus and served Him more perfectly, I praise Him for the grace given me to do more than in any former year of my life. I have written more, talked more, prayed more, and thought more for Jesus than in any previous year, and had more peace of mind, resulting from a stronger and more simple faith in Him. My realization of His presence and guidance has been deeper, fuller, and sweeter than ever before. In working for Jesus I have felt less burden, more perfect self-abandonment, more reliance on the blessed Spirit, and more conscious help from above, so I must call the year 1870 the best year of my life.[20]

With those feelings about 1870 in mind and recognizing that victorious living grew out of total commitment to God, Mary wrote "All for Jesus" as her resolution for 1871.

"All for Jesus" became Mary's best-known hymn. At least three people set it to music. The composer of the tune in *Sing to the Lord* is not known. Phineas Bresee, founder of the Church of the Nazarene, while protesting the "sentimental" songs of his day, used this hymn as an example of a hymn worthy of Christian worship.[21]

Mary James worked closely with Phoebe Palmer in the 19th-century Holiness Movement. For more information on Palmer, see pages 19-23.

FOR FURTHER READING

James, Joseph H. *The Life of Mrs. Mary D. James.* New York: Palmer and Hughes, 1886.

Fanny J. Crosby
(1820-1915)

Fanny Crosby stood before the Congress of the United States of America. No woman had ever addressed the distinguished body in its chambers until Fanny spoke there on January 24, 1844. She had traveled to Washington, D.C., with several students from the New York Institution for the Blind to lobby Congress for assistance. Blinded when just six weeks old by the improper treatment of an eye infection, she was a student at the Institution for the Blind for 8 years and a teacher for 15 years. As she stood before Congress, Fanny was a star attraction as the students demonstrated that blind people could achieve academic and artistic excellence in spite of their visual impairment. In her 13-stanza poem written for the occasion, she said:

> O ye who here from every State convene,
> Illustrious band! may we not hope the scene
> You now behold will prove to every mind
> Instruction hath a ray to cheer the blind.[22]

As her reputation as a poet spread, Fanny received opportunities to compose and recite her poetry at many civic events. She was the guest of U.S. Presidents Van Buren, Tyler, and Cleveland, and other federal and state dignitaries.

The musical doors were opened for Fanny by George Root, a music educator and composer. Root decided that musical plays might be teaching tools in the schools where he taught. Six years earlier, he had given music lessons at the New York Institution for the Blind. He remembered the talented Fanny Crosby and asked her to write lyrics for his musicals. George and Fanny eventually wrote many secular songs. One song, "Rosalie the Prairie Flower," provided a royalty of nearly $3,000, a large amount in the mid-1800s.[23]

In contrast to her standing as a celebrity, Fanny became increasingly aware that she was out of favor with God. Beginning in 1839, Fanny and several others from the school for the blind attended classes at the Eighteenth Street Methodist Church. A class leader from that congregation also held weekly meetings at the Institution for the Blind. So at least twice a week Fanny participated in Methodist class meetings, small groups designed to encourage spiritual formation. But Fanny did not have spiritual peace.

During 1850 the Thirtieth Street Methodist Church held revival meetings. Fanny and others from the Institution for the Blind attended. She wrote:

> On two occasions, I sought peace at the altar, but did not find the joy I craved, until one evening, November 20, 1850, it seemed to me that the light must indeed come then or never; and so I arose and went to the altar alone. After a prayer was offered, they began to sing the grand old consecration hymn,
>
> > "Alas, and did my Savior bleed,
> > And did my Sovereign die?"
>
> And when they reached the third line of the fourth stanza,
>
> > "Here Lord, I give myself away,"
>
> my very soul was flooded with a celestial light. I sprang to my feet, shouting "hallelujah," and then for the first time I realized that I had been trying to hold the world in one hand and the Lord in the other.[24]

Take the world, but give me Jesus;
All its joys are but a name,
But His love abideth ever,
Thro' eternal years the same.
Take the world, but give me Jesus;
In His cross my trust shall be,
Till, with clearer, brighter vision,
Face to face my Lord I see.

Fourteen years after her conversion Fanny wrote her first hymn. Once she started writing hymns at age 44, however, she became the most prolific gospel songwriter of all time. No one knows exactly how many hymns she wrote, partially because she often used noms de plume (pen names), but most hymnologists believe the total is over 8,000. For many years she was under contract with the Biglow and Main publishing company to provide 3 hymns each week, typically receiving $2 per song. Sometimes she would write as many 6 or 7 hymns in one day. In 1866, two years after she started writing hymns, composer Phillip Phillips sent Fanny 40 titles with the request that she write 40 hymns. Fanny composed all 40 songs before dictating them to a secretary.

Her first hymn was written with William Bradbury. Reflecting upon that initial effort, Fanny Crosby said that "it now seemed to me as if the great work of my life had really begun."[25] Relationships with other gospel song composers quickly developed. She worked with the most prominent church musicians in the 19th century: William Doane, William Kirkpatrick, Robert Lowry, George Stebbins, John Sweney, and others. Edmund Lorenz spoke of Doane and Lowry compiling songbooks "not as professional musicians, but as Christian workers."[26] That could be applied to the others as well. Fanny collaborated with men who were involved in ministry, not just in the music business.

Fanny Crosby was a talented musician: a soprano soloist, pianist, organist, harpist, and guitarist. She wrote hymn tunes but rarely allowed anyone to hear them. She believed her tunes were too complicated for congregational singing and preferred that others provide the tunes for her texts.

George Stebbins wrote, "There was probably no writer in her day who appealed more to the varied experiences of the Christian life or who expressed more sympathetically the deep longings of the human heart than Fanny Crosby."[27] People recognized the spiritual authenticity of her songs. For Fanny, a hymn was "a song of the heart addressed to God."[28]

> *Thou, my everlasting portion,*
> *More than friend or life to me,*
> *All along my pilgrim journey,*
> *Savior, let me walk with Thee.*

She disclosed that many of her hymns were "in response to a definite event in my own life."[29] Often she would write hymns at night as she reflected on the day. She needed the quietness of the night to sculpt her thoughts in rhyme. The mystical side of her poetic work was revealed when she wrote that "the most enduring hymns are born in the silences of the soul, and nothing must be allowed to intrude while they are being framed into language."[30]

Fanny wrote of her own spiritual pilgrimage in such a way that others recognized their own journeys in her words. Robert Lowry, her friend and colleague, wrote, "Not even the highest grade of poetry will secure a fixed place in the service of praise if it be lacking in spiritual quality. There must be in a hymn something which is readily apprehended by the Christian consciousness, coming forth from the experience of the writer, and clothed in strong and inspiring words, if it would hold its place as a permanent factor in Christian worship."[31] Fanny Crosby continues to be well-represented in hymnals printed decades after her death because she expressed her authentic spiritual experiences in hymns of the highest quality.

Surprisingly, Fanny did not see herself primarily as a hymn writer, especially in her later years. In an interview with the *New*

Haven Register,[32] she said that her first call was as a home mission worker.

Her work with men and women at risk started in 1871. Richard Morse, a Young Men's Christian Association worker Fanny knew, came to her early one morning asking if she had plans for the day. Fanny said her schedule was open. He then told her about an alcoholic who had attempted suicide. Richard had taken the man into his own room and given him something to eat. Richard asked Fanny to help him present the gospel to the man. They were effective evangelists that day. The man was redeemed and eventually became a minister.[33] After that Fanny Crosby became active in the YMCA, especially with the branches ministering to railroad workers.

Rescue the perishing;
Duty demands it.
Strength for thy labor
the Lord will provide.
Back to the narrow way
Patiently win them;
Tell the poor wand'rer
a Savior has died.

In 1881 Fanny started working with the Bowery Mission in New York City. She spoke at 16 anniversary services of this mission, writing a hymn for each one. She also often helped at the Water Street Mission. Sometimes she spoke, but usually she simply talked with the men and women, providing counsel and directing them to Christ. She was an untiring evangelist. She wrote, "There are many timid souls whom we jostle morning and evening as we pass them by; but if only the kind word were spoken they might become fully persuaded."[34]

Throughout her life, Fanny Crosby was concerned for others' welfare. In her younger days, while a teacher at the New York Institute for the Blind, she counseled Grover Cleveland. The future president of the United States was only 16 years old when his father died. Fanny Crosby helped him work through his grief. In her middle years Fanny often gave her money to those with greater needs. Some of her friends felt she was not properly compensated for her hymns. Ruffin, her biographer, believes that if she had received more money she would have given it away. On the night she died, just a month before her 95th birthday, she dictated a letter to a friend whose daughter had died. Fanny Crosby was a woman whose faith was expressed in kind acts and hymns of praise.

"To God Be the Glory" (*Sing to the Lord* No. 36)

"To God Be the Glory" was first published in 1875 but did not become widely used in the United States until the 1950s. Ira Sankey included it in his book *Sacred Songs and Solos,* which was published in England in the mid-1870s. The song became quite popular in that country. Cliff Barrows, crusade music director with the Billy Graham evangelistic team, heard the hymn for the first time while in England for a 1952 crusade. Two years later it was included in the songbook for Graham's 1954 London Crusade. The hymn was reintroduced in the United States at the next Billy Graham Crusade. Although forgotten in the United States for 80 years, this has become one of Fanny Crosby's most used hymns.[35]

"Hallelujah! Amen!" (*Sing to the Lord* No. 143)

Sing to the Lord lists Henrietta E. Blair as the author of this hymn. This nom de plume was one of more than 200 that Fanny Crosby used. Some of them were the names of real people, such as nieces and nephews she wanted to honor. Others were variations of her own name, such as her married name, Fanny Van Alstyne.[36]

Gospel hymn writers in the late 19th and early 20th centuries often used noms de plume. In Fanny's case, the pen names seemed to be used because of the tremendous volume of work she produced. The publishers apparently wanted to camouflage the fact that Fanny had written most of the songs in some of their books.

William Kirkpatrick wrote this hymn tune. Fanny Crosby first met "Kirkie" at the Holiness camp meeting in Ocean Grove, New Jersey, in 1877. Her relationship with him continued and she "visited Mr. Kirkpatrick at his home in Philadelphia several times."[37] Then she added, "I look back upon these occasions with peculiar pleasure."[38]

Kirkpatrick was converted as a teenager and became active in the Methodist Episcopal Church. Because of his musical abilities, while he was still a young man he transcribed camp meeting songs formerly passed through oral tradition. These songs became the basis for his first gospel song collection, *Devotional Melodies.* Kirkpatrick greatly influenced the music of the Wesleyan/Holiness Movement. Discussing the early hymnody of the Church of the Nazarene, Fred Mund wrote that Kirkpatrick's "influence was greatly felt through those early years. Although not a Nazarene, he did much to give the church a spiritual heritage from which it could grow."[39]

"Jesus Is Calling" (*Sing to the Lord* No. 322)

George Stebbins served as the music director for various congregations before he joined Dwight Moody in revivalistic efforts in 1876. He was a fine soloist and congregational song leader. For the next 25 years he worked with Moody and other well-known evangelists.

Of this invitation hymn, Stebbins said that neither the words nor the music impressed him "as possessing more than ordinary merit, even for evangelistic work. . . . That it would meet with instant favor, and in a few years would become generally known, did not enter my mind."[40]

"Pass Me Not" (*Sing to the Lord* No. 346)

One of Fanny's most productive relationships was with composer William Doane, who was an inventor and successful businessman. He patented 70 inventions and was the president of the J. A. Fay and Company, a manufacturer of woodworking equipment in Cincinnati. Doane was also an active Christian, working in Sunday Schools and compiling gospel songbooks. He composed about 2,300 tunes.

The second time Doane visited Fanny in New York City, he asked her to write a song using the phrase "Pass me not, O gentle Savior." She agreed to do so but didn't work on the project for several weeks. During the spring of 1868, while speaking at a prison in Manhattan, she heard an inmate cry out, "Good Lord, do not pass me by!" She immediately recalled the phrase Doane had given her. That evening in her room she wrote the hymn.[41]

"Blessed Assurance" (*Sing to the Lord* No. 442)

For many years Fanny Crosby was a member of the John Street Methodist Church of New York City. Another member of this congregation was Phoebe Palmer Knapp. Phoebe was the daughter of Walter and Phoebe Palmer, influential leaders of the American Holiness Movement. She married Joseph Knapp, founder of the Metropolitan Life Insurance Company, when she was just 16. An avocational musician, Knapp wrote about 500 hymn tunes.

While Fanny visited the Knapp mansion one day, Phoebe asked Fanny to listen to a tune she had written. After hearing the tune, Fanny clapped her hands and exclaimed, "Why, that melody says, 'Blessed assurance, Jesus is mine.'"[42] That hymn was soon completed and became one of the most widely used hymns authored by Fanny Crosby.

"I Am Thine, O Lord" (*Sing to the Lord* No. 473)

While on a speaking tour, Fanny stayed at William Doane's home in

Cincinnati. One evening they discussed God's nearness. As was often her custom, before going to sleep that night, Fanny wrote a new hymn, "I Am Thine, O Lord." Doane later wrote the melody.

Doane and Crosby worked well together. Once, while they traveled together by train from Cincinnati to New York, Doane whistled a melody to Fanny. She wrote words for the tune, which became, "Jesus, I love Thee, Thou art to me Dearer than mortal ever can be."[43]

"All the Way My Savior Leads Me" (*Sing to the Lord* No. 559)

Fanny Crosby chose to live in tenement sections of Lower Manhattan, even though many of her friends encouraged her to leave the slums. During the evenings she often invited her neighbors into her apartment where she would sing and play the guitar. Fanny gave money to these friends as they had need.

One day Fanny, herself, needed $5 to pay her rent and asked God to provide the money. Soon after her prayer, a man visited her. As he left, he shook hands with her, leaving a $5 bill in her hand. Fanny wrote: "I have no way to account for this, except to believe that God, in answer to my prayer, put it into the heart of this good man to bring me the money. My first thought, after finding out . . . was, 'In what a wonderful way the Lord helps me! All the way my Savior leads me!' I immediately wrote the hymn."[44]

This was the first hymn Fanny wrote with Robert Lowry, a pastor, hymn tune composer, and songbook compiler. Lowry wrote that he and Fanny had "many a conference on the phrasing of a hymn, and many a conversation on the phases of Christian experience."[45]

"Give Me Jesus" (*Sing to the Lord* No. 588)

One day Fanny was talking with a man who said, "If I had wealth, I would be able to do just what I wish to do and I would be able to make an appearance in the world." She immediately responded, "Take the world, but give me Jesus."[46] This spontaneous remark prompted her to write a hymn with that sentence as the first line.

John Sweney composed the tune for this text. Like Kirkpatrick, Fanny first met Sweney at Ocean Grove, New Jersey, in 1877. Besides being a popular music leader at camp meetings, Sweney composed about 1,000 songs. He compiled more than 60 songbooks—often collaborating with William Kirkpatrick.

"Saved by Grace" (*Sing to the Lord* No. 659)

Fanny Crosby attended a Methodist camp meeting at Poughkeepsie,

New York, in 1891. One of the speakers died a few days after Fanny heard him speak, while the camp was still in session. His sudden death caused many at the camp meeting to soberly consider eternal life. After a conversation with some friends, Fanny found a quiet place and wrote this hymn.

She sent the text to her primary publisher, Biglow and Main, but evidently it was filed and never assigned to a composer. A couple of years later, while attending Moody's Christian Workers' Conference in Northfield, Massachusetts, Ira Sankey asked Fanny to address the conference. She hesitated, but finally obliged. She closed her brief remarks with the poem "Saved by Grace."

A newspaper reporter from London printed the poem in an article about the conference. Sankey later sent a copy of the article to George Stebbins, asking that he set the poem to music. Stebbins complied and performed it for the first time at a revival meeting with Dwight Moody in Newport, Rhode Island.[47]

"My Savior First of All" (*Sing to the Lord* No. 662)

A minister once told Fanny that it was a shame that God had allowed her to be blind. Fanny never entertained this sentiment. When only eight years old she wrote:

> Oh, what a happy soul am I!
> Although I cannot see,
> I am resolved that in this world
> Contented I will be.

> How many blessings I enjoy
> That other people don't;
> To weep and sigh because I'm blind,
> I cannot, and I won't.[48]

Fanny shocked the minister with a rebuke. "Do you know that if at birth I had been able to make one petition to my Creator, it would have been that I should be born blind? When I get to heaven, the first face that shall ever gladden my sight will be that of my Savior."[49]

"Rescue the Perishing" (*Sing to the Lord* No. 713)

Not a few of my hymns have been written after experiences at the New York missions. One in particular has been used far and wide in evangelistic work. As I was addressing a large company of working men one hot August evening, the thought kept forcing itself upon my mind that some mother's boy must be rescued that very night or perhaps not at all. So I requested that, if there was any boy present, who had wandered away from mother's teaching, he would come to the platform at the conclusion of the service. A young man of eighteen came forward and said,

"Did you mean me? I have promised my mother to meet her in heaven; but as I am now living that will be impossible." We prayed for him; he finally arose with a new light in his eyes; and exclaimed triumphantly,

"Now, I can meet mother in heaven; for I have found her God."

A few days before, Mr. Doane had sent me the subject "Rescue the Perishing," and while I sat there that evening the line came to me,

"Rescue the perishing, care for the dying." I could think of nothing else that night. When I arrived at my home I went to work on it at once; and before I retired the entire hymn was ready for a melody.[50]

Fanny Crosby had a close relationship with the Palmer family: Walter, Phoebe, and Phoebe Palmer Knapp. For more information on the Palmers, see pages 19-23.

OTHER HYMNS BY FANNY J. CROSBY

"Praise Him! Praise Him!" (*Sing to the Lord* No. 117)
"Unsearchable Riches" (*Sing to the Lord* No. 140)
"Tell Me the Story of Jesus" (*Sing to the Lord* No. 205)
"Near the Cross" (*Sing to the Lord* No. 240)
"Redeemed" (*Sing to the Lord* Nos. 357 and 415)
"He Hideth My Soul" (*Sing to the Lord* No. 572)

FOR FURTHER READING

Crosby, Fanny J. *Bells at Evening and Other Verses,* 5th ed. New York: Biglow and Main Company, 1903.

———. *Fanny Crosby's Life-Story.* New York: Everywhere Publishing Company, 1903.

———. *Memories of Eighty Years.* Boston: James H. Earle, 1906.

Gosselin, Blanche. "She Hath Done What She Could." *Fundamentalist Journal* 7 (May 1988): 26-27, 35.

Hustad, Donald. *Fanny Crosby Speaks Again.* Carol Stream, Ill.: Hope Publishing Company, 1977.

Jackson, S. Trevena, and Sankey, I. Allan. *An Evening of Song and Story with Fanny J. Crosby.* New York: Biglow and Main, 1912.

Jackson, S. Trevena. *Fanny Crosby's Story of Ninety-Four Years.* New York: Fleming H. Revell Company, 1915.

Loveland, John. *Blessed Assurance: The Life and Hymns of Fanny J. Crosby.* Nashville: Broadman, 1978.

Murphree, J. Tal. "The American Lyricist: Strains of Holiness Theology in Crosby Hymns." *Holiness Digest* 4 (Fall 1990): 5-7.

Ruffin, Bernard. *Fanny Crosby.* Philadelphia: United Church Press, 1976.

Henry L. Gilmour
(1836-1920)

The voices resounding through the oak-timbered hills of Garrett County, Maryland, grew louder each hour. Some people came by train. Others by horse and buggy. A few who lived on local farms walked. The annual camp meeting at Mountain Lake Park wouldn't begin until the next day, but those who had already arrived gathered at Grace Cottage on Friday, July 6, 1894. They sang favorite hymns of praise and testimony such as: "Jesus, Lover of My Soul," "Oh, for a Heart to Praise My God," "The Haven of Rest," "Trust and Obey," and "He Leadeth Me." They quoted Scripture. They testified to God's grace in their lives. They prayed, fervently asking God to flood the camp meeting with the divine presence.[51]

Henry Lake Gilmour led the singing that evening. He also sang a solo. And he was the author of "The Haven of Rest," which the people sang. From 1885 into the 1900s Henry served as music director for the Mountain Lake Park camp meetings. His ministry was effective: "Where really helpful and spiritual music is desired . . . [Dr. Gilmour] is unsurpassed."[52]

Henry was born in Ireland. When 16 years old, he joined a ship's crew to learn navigation. When the ship landed in Philadelphia, however, Henry decided to seek his fortune. During the Civil War he was a member of the 1st New Jersey Cavalry, and he spent several months in the Confederate Libbey Prison. Following his discharge from the army, Henry enrolled in the Philadelphia Dental School and then worked as a dentist for many years.

But after he totally consecrated himself to God's will, his first love was his involvement in Christian ministry. For years, he spent his 10-week summer vacation going from camp meeting to camp meeting to assist with the music. He was a fine soloist and an engaging song leader and generally organized a choir at the camp meetings. For 40 years he led the choir at the Pitman Grove Camp Meeting. He frequently participated in the camp meetings at Ridgeview Park, Pennsylvania, and Ocean Grove, New Jersey.[53] During the rest of the year he often assisted with evening revival services after working as a dentist during the day.

During the 10 A.M. service on Saturday, July 14, at the 1894 Mountain Lake Park camp meeting, many people testified about their faith. Brother Smith, the emcee, called on Henry Gilmour to "take the witness stand." Henry was caught off guard but quickly testified:

> Such an opportunity as this is a surprise to me. I was not expecting to be called on, but I bless the Lord that I am always ready to witness for Him. I was converted at Cape May City. I had sought the Lord long and earnestly. The meetings had run for seven weeks, and the pastor said they must close. Another young man and myself were still at the altar, and Sister Hughes said that the meetings ought not to close until we were saved. But they said it involved too much expense to continue them longer, so they were moved to another place, and I continued to seek the Lord, struggling and singing and praying, but making no advancement. One night, on my way home from church to my boarding-house, a voice seemed to speak to me in such tones of love and compassion that I said in my soul, "I will stop all this struggling and trying right now, and just let you do it for me," and before I got home the joy of pardon came into my soul. Oh, I tell you I had a jubilee! My conversion was clear and satisfactory, and it lasted.[54]

O come to the Savior. He patiently waits
To save by His power divine.
Come, anchor your soul in the haven of rest,
And say, "My Beloved is mine."

Henry continued his testimony by saying that following his conversion "[my] wife and I were full of good works, and we found plenty to do, and the Lord blessed our labors." For example, the Methodist Church in Wenonah, New Jersey, began in their home. He served this congregation for many years as a church musician, Sunday School superintendent, Methodist class leader, and church trustee. He avidly promoted Holiness, often distributing Holiness periodicals and books.[55]

As Henry continued his testimony, he talked about the consecration of his musical talents.

> I was invited to Pitman Grove to sing. . . . The next year I was invited to take charge of the music there, and wife and I were both deeply convicted for holiness. So, one day when a

young lady singer led the way we followed, and the whole choir was soon down in the straw seeking full salvation. While I knelt there the music question confronted me, and I asked where I should draw the line. Brother Inskip replied, "Let the Holy Ghost draw the line." I said, "Yes, I will," and immediately the light came in. That was the only thing over which I had any struggle at the time of my consecration for holiness, for my tobacco and other evil habits had gone long before. But the music question had to be settled, and when I turned it over to the Holy Ghost for settlement I soon understood that henceforth I was to sing for Jesus only. As soon as I agreed to that I came into liberty.[56]

Henry had been saved and sanctified wholly. But one more spiritual experience prepared him for the music ministry to which God had called him. While at a camp meeting at Mountain Lake Park he was "consciously empowered . . . for service."[57] Henry ended his testimony by noting the extent of his spiritual experience. "It is just the same in my home, in my business, wherever I am, I am just as happy as I am in these meetings. Oh, I find full salvation good everywhere, and all the time. Hallelujah!"[58]

Beyond Henry's own ministry as a soloist and song leader, he involved others in the ministry of music. During the first day of the 1894 Mountain Lake Park camp meeting, Henry organized a choir. The

> *He brought me out of the miry clay;*
> *He set my feet on the Rock to stay.*
> *He puts a song in my soul today,*
> *A song of praise, hallelujah!*

record read, "Already our 'song prince,' Dr. Gilmour, has gathered around him an excellent choir (which he has a peculiar talent for doing), and the song service was inspiring."[59] Henry's daughter, Pauline, was a trained musician and often assisted her father. "Miss Gilmour is our faithful and efficient organist, who for years has helped greatly to make this meeting what it is, by the untiring assistance she has afforded her father in the service of song."[60]

Henry collaborated with several people in writing gospel songs. He also acted as an agent for the printing and promotion of other writers' songs, such as Lelia Morris. He compiled 16 songbooks, occasionally working with William Kirkpatrick.

On Friday, July 2, 1897, at 7:30 P.M., the people who arrived a day early for the annual Mountain Lake Park camp meeting gathered to sing and testify and read scripture. They begin by singing

"The Comforter Has Come." "Dr. Gilmour and family are present, and the music, as usual, is inspiring."[61] When Dr. Gilmour sang, he did so "like a man on fire of the Holy Ghost."[62] Henry had been transformed by God, and his spiritual vitality made his music alive.

"The Haven of Rest" (*Sing to the Lord* No. 409)

La Penna stated that "The Haven of Rest" was written during a camp meeting at Ocean Grove, New Jersey, in which Henry Gilmour assisted with the music.[63] Given the location of Ocean Grove on the Atlantic and the nautical metaphor used in the hymn, this claim is plausible, but not confirmed by other sources. The music was written by George D. Moore, an itinerant evangelist in New Jersey and Pennsylvania in the late 1800s.[64]

"He Brought Me Out" (*Sing to the Lord* No. 412)

Amanda Smith, an African-American evangelist, spoke at many Holiness camp meetings in the late 19th and early 20th centuries. She dramatically told of being freed twice, from slavery and sin. Henry Zelley and Henry Gilmour both attended a camp meeting where Amanda Smith preached. After hearing her speak, Zelley and Gilmour wrote two of their best-known songs, "He Brought Me Out" and "He Rolled the Sea Away" (*Sing to the Lord* No. 649).[65] Amanda Smith, who was also a fine soloist, wrote four additional stanzas for the song "He Rolled the Sea Away" and sang them at the 1901 General Holiness Convention in Chicago.[66]

Henry Gilmour was instrumental in the publication of the songs of Lelia Morris. For more information on Morris, see pages 46-49.

Clara T. Williams
(1858-1937)

The Saturday morning sun warmed Clara as she urged her horse to begin their weekly journey. She had arranged for her elderly, infirm father to care for himself while she was away. Being early summer she didn't have to worry about inclement weather.

For several months in 1894 Clara Tear served a Wesleyan Methodist circuit in Ohio. On Saturday mornings she drove her horse and buggy 20 miles to Middlefield, where she stayed in a partially furnished house provided by the Middlefield congregation. After preaching at the Sunday morning worship service, Clara would travel 10 miles to Windsor Mills, where she conducted a Sunday evening service. On Monday morning she traveled the 15 miles to the home she shared with her father. After caring for him all week she repeated the circuit the next weekend.[67]

Although never ordained, Clara was a licensed minister in the Wesleyan Methodist Church. For many years she traveled as an evangelist and occasionally served as an interim pastor. For five years she pastored the Pine Grove, Pennsylvania, circuit where one Sunday she preached at Dixonville and Hillsdale and the next at Rich Hill and Spruce.

The Tear family was firmly Wesleyan in belief and practice. Clara's great-grandfather had heard John Wesley preach during at least one of Wesley's tours of the Isle of Man. When the Tear family settled in Lake County, Ohio, in 1826, they joined the Methodist Episcopal Church. Clara grew up in a home offering Methodist classics and the *Guide to Holiness*.

Clara was converted at the age of 13 and wrote, "I was impressed that I was taking the wrong road, that my heart was growing hard, and if I did not soon submit to God I would be forever lost."[68] The growing conviction found resolution during an evening service at the Methodist church. "Sitting back in the old home church one night, the matter was settled, and as I started up the aisle toward the altar, the love of God came into my heart."[69] Clara considered that night as the turning point in her life.

When she was 17 years old, Clara realized the need for a further work of God in her life. With her parents, Clara attended a meeting held by "some Holiness people." Again God touched her. She wrote, "I knew my need and accepted an invitation to the altar, with no apparent result. As we drove from the church and I looked back at the unworldly appearing workers as they stood on the platform in front, . . . the question came forcibly, would I be willing to give up the world with its fashions and pleasures and fully follow the Lord? My heart responded 'Yes' and there flowed through my being a flood of glory that was inexpressible."[70]

Hallelujah! I have found Him,
Whom my soul so long has craved!
Jesus satisfies my longings;
Through His blood I now am saved.

While Clara believed that God had cleansed her heart at that moment, she didn't tell anyone about it. But God continued to transform Clara before she was ready to begin her public ministry.

A few months after her sanctification, Clara attended another Holiness meeting with her parents. She recalled: "As we entered the church, the congregation was singing that familiar hymn 'I Need Thee Every Hour.' Through the song the Holy Spirit burnt into my soul my awful need of *His abiding presence.* I remember little else about the service; but from that time I knew what it was to 'hunger and thirst after righteousness' and could think of little else."[71] But God had a still deeper work in store for Clara's soul in the next week:

> While I had given myself to the Lord, it now seemed infinitely more to consent to His taking possession and control of my entire being. I had already taught a term of district school and my ambition was to make teaching my life work. I would earn enough by teaching in country schools to enable me to secure a fine education. I could dress well and be able to associate with nice, intelligent people. Now if I abandoned myself to the Lord and took my hands off, He might lead otherwise. Was I willing to be separate from this proud, wicked world and live only to please God? To be like Him, despised and rejected of men? It seemed for two days and nights I could not say yes. The suggestion came that I had at times been much blessed of the Lord and had been living a good life. Why not be content? But it was very clear that to draw back meant darkness and perdition.

On the following Tuesday I returned to the meetings. As I sat in the evening service I came to a point where the matter had to be settled, and finally my heart said, "Perish every fond ambition, all I've sought or hoped or know." I died to the world and self. Faith was spontaneous. When there was a request for those to stand who had received the cleansing I rose to my feet and as I did so the glory came.[72]

God's work in Clara's heart brought an immediate change. She was formerly timid about discussing God; now she freely testified of God's grace. Before this experience she never prayed in public; that fear disappeared.

Very soon after this spiritual experience, Clara heard God's call to a preaching ministry. On three successive days God brought to her mind John 15:16, "Ye have not chosen me, but I have chosen you, and ordained you, that ye should go and bring forth fruit, and that your fruit should remain" (KJV).

However, instead of immediately following the Lord's directive to preach, Clara accepted a teaching position. She taught only a few weeks that year because tuberculosis infected her body. After her recovery another school offered her a teaching position. Clara promised to respond in a few days. But she didn't need that long to decide. She wrote, "I went to my room and my knees, when the Lord said to me, 'Haven't I told you what I want you to do? Why pray?' I immediately went out and gave my answer to the man who had not yet driven out of the yard."[73]

Clara began her public ministry in 1883 as a companion to Sister Mary DePew, a well-known evangelist in the Wesleyan Methodist Church. Her travels would take her from Iowa to New York during the next 20 years. After her marriage to William H. Williams in 1895, she worked with her husband in several pastoral assignments.

Clara spent her last years in Houghton, New York, where George Beverly Shea lived at the time. Shea remembers meeting the elderly Clara Tear Williams while he was a young boy. He wrote: "She had a regal and dignified bearing and yet she had the kindness and gentleness of Christ in her face. When I came to know her and often spoke with her, I enjoyed the soft, musical tones of her voice. Through her sweetness and graciousness to everyone, she became another wonderful proof to me of the reality of the Christian walk."[74]

Clara Tear Williams was a living example of the beauty God creates in the totally consecrated person.

"Satisfied" (*Sing to the Lord* No. 383)

Even though "Satisfied" was not published until 1881, it was written near 1875, when Clara was 18 years old, according to her unpublished autobiography. She wrote: "I think I had been saved about four years and was helping in meetings on the charge of Rev. Hunscher in Troy, Ohio, where Professor R. E. Hudson conducted the singing, when just before retiring one night, the latter asked me to write a song for a book he was preparing to publish. Before sleeping I wrote 'Satisfied.' In the morning he composed the music."[75]

Following his honorable discharge from the army after the Civil War, Ralph Hudson taught music at Mount Vernon College in Alliance, Ohio. He was known as "Professor" even after he left the college to devote himself to evangelism and music publishing. Hudson was a licensed preacher in the Methodist Episcopal Church. Besides writing the music for "Satisfied," Hudson wrote the words for "I'll Live for Him" (*Sing to the Lord* No. 497) and the words and music for "His Yoke Is Easy" (*Sing to the Lord* No. 411) and "A Glorious Church" (*Sing to the Lord* No. 672).

Clara Williams was a respected "saint" in the church of George Beverly Shea's childhood. For more information on Shea, see pages 82-85.

FOR FURTHER READING

Clara Tear Williams Collection, William J. Houghton Library, Houghton College, Houghton, New York.
"Obituary for Clara Tear Williams." *The Wesleyan Methodist* 95 (July 28, 1937): 14.
"Passing of a Saint." *The Wesleyan Methodist* 95 (July 28, 1937): 2.

Lelia N. Morris
(1862-1929)

The speaker preached on repentance at the Sunday morning service of the 1898 Mountain Lake Park camp meeting. A woman who responded to the invitation struggled as she prayed at the altar. Being a person of means, she wanted to give something to God for her salvation, not simply receive the gift of God's grace. Lelia Morris quietly knelt beside the woman and began to pray. Soon Henry Gilmour, the camp meeting song leader, and the preacher, Rev. L. H. Baker, joined them.

As they prayed with the woman, Lelia said, "Just now your doubting give o'er." Gilmour added, "Just now reject Him no more." Then Baker said, "Just now throw open the door." Lelia completed the thought, "Let Jesus come into your heart." Lelia noted the spontaneous phrases and wove them into a new song, "Let Jesus Come into Your Heart," which she completed at the camp meeting.[76]

Lelia loved to attend camp meetings. Beginning in 1892, she regularly traveled to Maryland for the annual Mountain Lake Park camp meeting. Some of her best-loved songs were written there: "I Know God's Promise Is True" (*Sing to the Lord* No. 367), "Sweet Will of God" (*Sing to the Lord* No. 462), and "Holiness unto the Lord" (*Sing to the Lord* No. 503). She also routinely attended Holiness camp meetings in her home state: Sebring Camp in Sebring, Ohio, and Old Camp Sychar in Mount Vernon, Ohio. Although she seemed able to write a song at any time and any place, she said the camp meetings were so inspiring "that she was able to write better after she returned" home.[77]

Lelia wrote her first song soon after attending her first Mountain Lake Park camp meeting, while she sewed a garment for one of her children. She wrote: "I was stitching on my machine and singing at my work. Suddenly I realized that I was singing a message from my heart. I walked over to the piano and played it. From that time on I have written and played little hymns. New songs crowded into my mind, four or five in a day. You just would not believe how fast they came."[78]

Apprehensive about what people might say if they knew she wrote songs, Lelia hid her early efforts. When an idea came, she would write it down and put it away. One day she mentioned this to her mother, who asked Lelia to sing some of the songs. Lelia's mother told her the songs were special gifts from God. She took one of them to the choir leader at their church, who recognized the song's quality. An evangelist who was holding revival meetings in town persuaded Lelia to take her songs to Mountain Lake Park.

After Henry Gilmour published them in his songbooks, people all over the country, and eventually around the world, started singing the songs of an Ohio housewife. Lelia wrote about 1,500 songs.

O magnify the Lord with me,
Ye people of His choice.
Let all to whom He lendeth breath
Now in His name rejoice.
For love's blest revelation,
For rest from condemnation,
For uttermost salvation,
To Him give thanks.

Lelia was converted when she was 10 years old. She wrote, "Three different years I went forward to the altar and prayed and prayed, until a man came and laid his hand on my head and said, 'Why, little girl, God is here and ready to forgive your sins.'"[79]

About the same time Lelia began piano lessons, faithfully practicing at a neighbor's house. When she was 12 or 13 she began playing the reed organ for prayer meetings at the Methodist church she attended.

At the 1892 Mountain Lake Park camp meeting Lelia heard Holiness preached for the first time. She was stirred by the preachers' words about a clean heart: "I read in books about the Holy Spirit and how that we might have the Holy Spirit come into our lives. I had read this over and over again, but thought it was for bishops and preachers and those doing great work for God. I did not suppose it was for me. Only did I find out in the preaching that it was for the young, such as I."[80]

Lelia evidently did not receive the "second blessing" at the camp meeting. After she returned home Rev. James L. Glascock, a Methodist evangelist, held a Holiness tent revival in her hometown. There, Lelia was sanctified. This spiritual experience "opened up to her the lifework that has made her a blessing, not only to her own home and church circle, but to countless millions of people."[81]

When asked how she could find the time to write so many songs while caring for her husband and four children, she replied: "Oh, I get both words and music when I am about my household tasks, and then when I have a little time I am ready to write them down. My housework is just routine work and I don't need to give it thought. I wouldn't get much done if I didn't get my songs ready to be written down when I am mopping my floor or washing dishes."[82]

In a short biography of Lelia Morris, Mary Ethel Wiess wrote that Lelia's songs "were not mere words written to fit music, but they were the expressions of her soul; and those who knew her felt them to be so."[83] Charles Gabriel wrote that Lelia "lived a consecrated Christian life, believing . . . that if she would write a noble poem, she must first live a noble life."[84] Lelia Morris was a housewife who had been touched by God and expressed the wonder of spiritual life through her songs.

"Sweeter As the Years Go By" (*Sing to the Lord* No. 397)

Lelia wrote this hymn in 1912. Speaking of Jesus' earthly ministry, the second stanza says in part, "He healed the brokenhearted, and caused the blind to see." She did not know her eyesight would begin to fail the next year. By 1914 she was totally blind.

This did not prevent Lelia from writing songs. While she still had some sight, her son installed a 28-foot chalkboard in her home on which a music staff was drawn. She wrote the notes of her tunes on the chalkboard and someone else would transcribe them to paper. After she lost all vision, she learned to touch-type her poems, then dictate the melodies to her daughter. Amazingly, Lelia always remembered the tunes until her daughter's annual visit.

Lelia wrote "'Tis Marvelous and Wonderful" (*Sing to the Lord* No. 406) five years after she became totally blind. The third stanza of this hymn states:

> From glory to glory He leads me on,
> From grace to grace ev'ry day;
> And brighter and brighter the glory dawns
> While pressing my homeward way,
> While pressing my homeward way.

The difficult circumstances of life did not dampen Lelia's spirits. She testified that "Jesus' love is sweeter, sweeter as the years go by."

"Holiness unto the Lord" (*Sing to the Lord* No. 503)

Wiess wrote that Lelia "had a sincere and strong belief in the subject of holiness, and she was well acquainted with all the Bible references on that subject. She made that a special subject of study and was a willing and ready speaker on that topic."[85] This song was written during the 1900 Mountain Lake Park Holiness camp meeting. Another Holiness hymn by Lelia Morris in the *Sing to the Lord* hymnal is "Sanctifying Power" (*Sing to the Lord* No. 509).

"Holiness unto the Lord" has become the unofficial theme song of the Church of the Nazarene.

Lelia Morris was encouraged in her songwriting efforts by Henry Gilmour. For more information on Gilmour, see pages 38-41.

OTHER HYMNS BY LELIA N. MORRIS

"Let All the People Praise Thee" (*Sing to the Lord* No. 61)
"Bring Your Vessels, Not a Few" (*Sing to the Lord* No. 294)
"I Know God's Promise Is True" (*Sing to the Lord* No. 367)
"'Tis Marvelous and Wonderful" (*Sing to the Lord* No. 406)
"Sweet Will of God" (*Sing to the Lord* No. 462)
"Nearer, Still Nearer" (*Sing to the Lord* No. 478)
"Sanctifying Power" (*Sing to the Lord* No. 509)
"Victory All the Time" (*Sing to the Lord* No. 648)

FOR FURTHER READING

Wiess, Mary Ethel. *Singing at Her Work: A Biography of Mrs. C. H. Morris.* Kansas City: Nazarene Publishing House, 1934, 1953.

Charles P. Jones
(1865-1949)

In 1865, the year of Charles Price Jones's birth, the 13th Amendment to the Constitution of the United States was ratified. African-Americans like Charles welcomed the amendment that abolished slavery, but the harsh realities of poverty and prejudice continued. Charles's mother died while he was still a teenager. He had poor health. In his autobiography he wrote, "I had a spell of sickness nearly every year and was so afflicted as not to hope to reach my thirtieth year."[86]

Following his mother's death, Charles set out on his own. Just 17 years old, he left Texas Valley, Georgia, traveling in his home state, then to Tennessee and Arkansas. In the Locust Grove Baptist Church at Cat Island, Arkansas, Charles was converted in 1884. The next year, Charles started preaching the gospel and eventually became known as an effective communicator. Charles was a very popular pastor and evangelist who spoke with great power.

As has often been the case in church history, Charles Jones's effectiveness attracted detractors as well as converts. In 1897 Charles's preaching was interrupted by gunfire. Five people were shot but not seriously injured.

A short time later in another city, Charles used Isa. 32:1-2 as his text, "Behold, a king shall reign in righteousness, and princes shall rule in judgment. And a man shall be as an hiding place from the wind, and a covert from the tempest; as rivers of water in a dry place, as the shadow of a great rock in a weary land" (KJV). As Charles invited people to respond to the gospel by kneeling at an altar for prayer, "a white bootlegger shot at [him] five or six times."[87] No one was injured this time. A comrade in crime killed the sniper the next day. No minister in the city would conduct the man's funeral since he had "interfered with that colored man's meetings, and had no business to do it."[88]

In 1905 Charles Jones pastored a congregation where as many as 1,200 people gathered met is a building situated on a steep hillside. Posts about six feet high supported the downhill side of the building. Gathering at the exposed underside of the building, a "mob got coal oil and set the meeting house on fire . . . a piece of malicious vandalism."[89] The mob prevented others from putting the fire out. The next day friends, both black and white, made contributions to help the congregation rebuild.

These physical challenges of safety were companions of Charles's spiritual battles. While Charles was the pastor of the Tabernacle Baptist Church in Selma, Alabama, he felt he needed "a deeper experience of grace, a larger power."[90] After fasting and praying for three days, God "sanctified me sweetly in His love. . . . The earnestness of the Spirit was mine. . . . The blessing of God rested upon me—all on the merits of Jesus. For in myself I felt more unworthy and undone than ever. It was the nearness, the eminence, the reality of the presence of God that exalted my spirit and filled me with joy, the joy of the Holy Ghost. Yet it made me feel keenly my unworthiness and the daily need of 'amazing grace.'"[91]

> *Deeper, deeper!*
> *though it cost hard trials,*
> *Deeper let me go!*
> *Rooted in the holy love of Jesus,*
> *Let me fruitful grow.*

Writing about this experience 41 years later, Charles said he gave himself to the Lord to be sanctified because he "wanted to be personally holy."[92]

Charles soon was convinced that everyone needed this sanctification. He wanted others to know the spiritual assurance that resulted from a heart made pure by the refining fire of God's Spirit. Charles started challenging people to consecrate themselves wholly to God. He urged them to "get the real experience of the fullness of the Spirit."[93]

The burden to proclaim Holiness led to Charles's ministry as a songwriter.

One day as I staggered under the weight of this obligation, under the necessity of this ministry, I felt that I must be alone and especially talk with God about it. I went to the home of Sister Rachel Williams, a God-fearing woman, the widow of Deacon Ben Williams, and asked if I might lock myself in her parlor and remain unmolested till I had reached the Lord with this matter. Oh the relief and help possible through prayer. It is good when burdened to pray it out; some phrase it "pray through." I prayed from about 9 a.m. to about 3 p.m. This was the burden of my prayer: "Lord, give me power to convince my people and my generation of the beauty of holiness and the advantages of righteousness" (Deut. 28). My people loved beauty, but the beauty of the flesh is vain and deceiving and soon passes. They wanted to advance in the world; but worldly advantages proved only a snare; for wealth promotes robbery, engenders pride and breeds strife; which to my people was fatal. I saw that in God was our salvation temporal and eternal. I desired that they should see it. . . . And so I prayed. Between 3 and 4 o'clock in the afternoon I became exhausted. I lay down on the sofa on which I knelt and said, "Lord, I'm exhausted. I can pray no more." Then the Lord flooded me with blessing. . . . My vision was clarified, my eyes were opened. . . . Surely the heavens were opened. The Spirit spoke within from the holy of holies of my redeemed spirit, and said, "You shall write the hymns for your people." This He said six or seven times till it was fixed in my mind. I got up and went to the organ in the corner of the room, wrote a song titled "Praise the Lord," ruled off a tablet, set it to music, and sang it before I left the room.[94]

Charles Jones eventually wrote more than 1,000 gospel songs. According to his own testimony, "most of them [were] born out of significant experiences—experiences of trial or of victory or both."[95]

In June 1897 Charles organized a "colored" Holiness convention for participants from Arkansas, Tennessee, Missouri, Illinois, North Carolina, Louisiana, Alabama, and Georgia. A second Holiness convention occurred the following year. These conventions were interdenominational, but many of the people eventually joined a new denomination, the Church of Christ (Holiness) U.S.A., in which Charles Price Jones was bishop.

"I Would Not Be Denied" (*Sing to the Lord* No. 390)

One time Charles Jones believed he should not serve Communion to his congregation because "the church was not in a good condition of spiritual unity."[96] The deacons, however, insisted that he serve Communion, so Charles acquiesced. This launched a personal spiritual battle since Charles felt he disobeyed God in doing so. He fasted and prayed, "yet fears distressed me and the consolations of the Spirit were denied me, or seemed to be."[97]

Having been rebuked, I refused to be comforted. But oh, how I prayed in every closet, behind every door; wherever I could hide I went to my knees begging for mercy. But no comfort came. You who have been tried in spirit can understand this. Satan tempted me to despair. . . . Then one night I was given a "song in the night." The room seemed filled with angels.

... My mourning became a song. When all the trial was over, thinking of it all one day while alone communing with God and thanking Him for His mercy to me, my soul felt that it must express itself in song; and so was born "I Would Not be Denied." Out of the depths I had come. Grace had triumphed. My soul sang unto the Lord a new song.[98]

"Deeper, Deeper" (*Sing to the Lord* No. 475)

Charles was bewildered while meditating on the promise in John 14:12 that the believer will do greater works than Jesus. Could a humble believer perform miracles that are greater than those of Jesus? And if so, Charles wondered, why were his own exploits so puny? His dissatisfaction with his limited ability made Charles realize he needed a "deeper grace, deeper wisdom, more perfect conformity to and willingness to do God's will."[99] As Charles pondered his plight, God gave him a song through which he expressed his prayer for spiritual growth.

FOR FURTHER READING

Blumhofer, Edith L. "'Jesus Only,' The Ministry of Charles Price Jones." *Assemblies of God Heritage* 7 (Spring 1987): 14-15.

Cobbins, Otho B. *History of Church of Christ (Holiness) U.S.A. 1895-1965*. New York: Vantage Press, 1966.

Jones, Charles Price. "Autobiographical Sketch of Charles Price Jones Founder of the Church of Christ (Holiness) U.S.A." *The Journal of Black Sacred Music* 2 (Fall 1988): 52-59.

————. "Inductive Lessons in Vocal Music." *The Journal of Black Sacred Music* 2 (Fall 1988): 81-82.

————. "The History of My Songs." *The Journal of Black Sacred Music* 2 (Fall 1988): 60-80.

Spencer, Jon Michael. "Jesus Only, Nos. 1 and 2: A Review." *The Journal of Black Sacred Music* 2 (Fall 1988): 83-87.

————. "The Hymnody of Charles Price Jones and the Church of Christ (Holiness) USA." *Black Sacred Music* 4 (Fall 1990): 14-29.

Thomas O. Chisholm
(1866-1960)

Thomas described it as "the darkest day of my life." As he stood before his mother's grave he asked "the undertaker to let her precious body down to its resting-place tenderly."[100] He had lived alone with his mother and with her death had to move from the house they had shared. But of greater importance, he realized his own mortality and needy spiritual condition.

Two years after his mother's death, Thomas attended revival services in Franklin, Kentucky, where Henry Clay Morrison was the evangelist. Morrison was a highly esteemed member of the National Association for the Promotion of Holiness and spoke with great power. During the service Thomas felt the convicting power of the Holy Spirit. After the revival meeting he went "to his own room and with almost a feeling of despair, read the eighteenth chapter of John. It records Jesus' arrest in the garden and His being led forth to die. Into Chisholm's mind flashed the thought that he, as much as any other, perhaps more, had made necessary this tragedy."[101] With the extent of his sin in mind, he also began to see the breadth of God's grace. There in his room he found the glory of forgiveness. "He felt as though he had passed out of a long dark tunnel into bright sunlight. He had such an experience of salvation that he never questioned its reality."[102]

Although he never graduated from high school, at 16 Thomas began teaching at the country school he had attended. The publisher of the local weekly newspaper, *The Franklin Favorite*, noted

O to be like Thee! Lord I am coming,
Now to receive th'anointing divine.
All that I am and have I am bringing;
Lord, from this moment all shall be Thine.

Thomas's writing skills, and at the age of 21 he began work as an editor.

As a new Christian he used his writing talents to advance the gospel. Soon after Thomas's conversion in 1893, H. C. Morrison asked him to move to Louisville to become office manager and editor of *The Pentecostal Herald*. Ten years later he was ordained as a Methodist minister and pastored the Methodist congregation in Scottsville, Kentucky. His pastoral service, however, was short-lived; he left Scottsville in less than a year because of health problems. Thomas moved his family to Winona Lake, Indiana, where he sold life insurance. In 1916 they moved to Vineland, New Jersey, where he continued to sell insurance.

Meanwhile, Chisholm continued to provide pastoral care through his poems. Using his own journey as a seedbed, he brought flowers of hope to others. He told Charles Gabriel, "Having been led, for a part of my life, through some difficult paths, I have sought to gather from such experiences material out of which to write hymns of comfort and cheer for those similarly circumstanced."[103]

He spent His life in doing good;
I want to be like Jesus.
In lowly paths of service trod;
I want to be like Jesus.
He sympathized with hearts distressed,
He spoke the words that cheered and blessed,
He welcomed sinners to His breast.
*I want to be like Jesus.**

On another occasion he wrote, "I have sought to be true to the Word, and to avoid flippant and catchy titles and treatment. I have greatly desired that each hymn or poem might have some definite message to the hearts for whom it was written."[104]

Thomas sent his poems to leading gospel songwriters of the day. He appreciated the critique and encouragement he received from Fanny Crosby. His texts were set to tunes by William Kirkpatrick, Haldor Lillenas, Bertha Mae Lillenas, Henry Gilmour, George Stebbins, John Sweney, David Ives, and others. Besides his hymns, scores of his poems were published in leading Christian periodicals such as *The Sunday School Times, Moody Monthly*, and the *Herald of Holiness*. In all, Thomas wrote more than 1,200 poems.

Thomas never made much money from his creative work or insurance sales. In a letter from 1941 he wrote: "My income has not been large at any time due to impaired health in the earlier years which has followed me on until now. Although I must not fail to

---

record here the unfailing faithfulness of a covenant-keeping God and that He has given me many wonderful displays of His providing care, for which I am filled with astonishing gratefulness."[105] In spite of his poverty, his life illustrated the spiritual richness our faithful God provides.

"Great Is Thy Faithfulness" (*Sing to the Lord* No. 44)

During the summer of 1955, James Draper led songs for the Moody Bible Institute Alumni Bible Conference in Ocean Grove, New Jersey. "Great Is Thy Faithfulness" was Moody Bible Institute's unofficial theme song and was sung at the alumni gathering. Thomas Chisholm, who was then retired and living in Ocean Grove, attended and was introduced to the congregation.

After the service, Draper asked Chisholm how the hymn had been written. Thomas said that "he had been reading Lamentations 3:22-23 and was suddenly overwhelmed with the mercy and faithfulness of God. He indicated that the words came quickly and exactly expressed the fullness of his heart."[106] No specific circumstance led to Thomas writing the song, just a general awareness that God had been faithful throughout his life.

When Thomas wrote "Great Is Thy Faithfulness" in 1923, he sent it with several other poems to William Runyan, a Methodist pastor, evangelist, and music editor. Runyan set Chisholm's text to music. For many years Runyan taught at Moody Bible Institute and served as a music editor for Hope Publishing Company.

"I Want to Be Like Jesus" (*Sing to the Lord* No. 208)

In 1945, while collecting material for a gospel songbook, David Livingstone Ives received several poems from Thomas Chisholm. David wrote that "two of the poems especially appealed to me at the time. One of them was 'I Want to Be Like Jesus,' which seemed to sing itself almost at the first reading."[107] Chisholm approved of the musical setting, telling David that it was a "perfect marriage of words and music."

"O to Be Like Thee" (*Sing to the Lord* No. 490)

Thomas Chisholm wrote this hymn after reading Hannah Whitall Smith's book *A Christian's Secret of a Happy Life.* This book caused Thomas to yearn for a deeper religious experience, which resulted in this poem.[108]

Thomas sent this poem and others to William Kirkpatrick, the most prominent songbook editor in the 19th-century Holiness

Movement. Kirkpatrick set the poem to music and published it in 1897. This was Chisholm's first song to be widely circulated.

"Living for Jesus" (*Sing to the Lord* No. 496)

In 1915 Harold Lowden wrote a "light and summery" gospel song to be sung by children. The song became quite popular and several pastors suggested a general text might make the song more useful. As Lowden considered their suggestions, he felt the melody suggested the phrase "Living for Jesus." So he sent Thomas Chisholm a copy of the music, requesting that Thomas write a lyric with that title. Lowden said Chisholm "returned it to me, saying he didn't have the slightest idea as to the method used in writing words to music. Immediately I sent the material back to him, telling him I believed God had led me to select him."[109] Since Thomas could not read music, he asked his daughter to hum the melody over and over until he was able to write the text of this hymn.[110]

––––––––––––

Thomas Chisholm cherished the encouragement he received early in his hymn writing career from Fanny Crosby. For more information on Crosby, see pages 28-37. Thomas sent hymns to many composers, including Henry Gilmour (see pages 38-41), Haldor Lillenas (see pages 69-76), and David Ives (see pages 90-93).

FOR FURTHER READING

Chisholm, Thomas O. *Great Is Thy Faithfulness and Other Song Lyrics and Poems.* Vineland, N.J.: Glendale Press, 1956.

Clark, Suzanna. "Songs of an Unsung Servant." *Hymn Lovers' Magazine* 5 (July / August 1951): 14-15, 37.

Annie Johnson Flint
(1866-1932)

Two visitors knocked on the door, asking to see Annie. The nurse, concerned about the frail, 65-year-old woman under her care, refused to let them in. When Annie heard of this she called for her visitors. As the guests entered the room they saw a small, frail woman lying in bed, supported by several pillows. For 40 years arthritis had made every move a painful struggle. Now Annie was practically paralyzed, her joints locked. Those who saw her never forgot her knotted hands: fingers tangled and wrists warped.

Annie's life had always been difficult. Her mother died when Annie was 3 years old, soon after the birth of her sister. Her father, Eldon Johnson, sent his two daughters to stay with the widow of a Civil War comrade. But this woman had few resources and two children of her own. The two Johnson children were unwelcome and sometimes neglected. A neighbor, aware of the dire circumstances, introduced Eldon to Mr. and Mrs. Flint. The Flints had no children and agreed to adopt the girls. Eldon approved the arrangements because the Flints were Christians. About a year later Eldon died. When Annie was in her early 20s her adoptive parents died. Shortly before their deaths Annie started having trouble with arthritis. Annie's sister was not well and could not care for her. At 23 Annie was unable to continue working as a teacher and was left without financial support and personal care.

Despite the physical turmoil, spiritual peace stabilized Annie's life. When Annie was 8 years old, the Flints moved to Vineland, New Jersey, where a Methodist church conducted revival meetings. "During one of these meetings . . . the Spirit of God operated upon that young heart and brought her to saving faith in Christ."[111]

In later years some people told Annie they believed children could not grasp spiritual truth. Annie vigorously disagreed. "She felt that the divine mysteries were often plainer to the simple faith of a child than to many adults, blinded by their own prejudices and intellectual doubts."[112]

Her conversion was the beginning of a life of growth in grace.

Annie believed "that Christians should go on, ever on, experimentally, into the truth of God. Taking the words of Paul, 'Therefore, leaving the first principles let us go on unto perfection,' she wrote a poetic incitement under the title, 'Let Us Go On.'"[113] The first stanza reads:

> Some of us stay at the cross,
> Some of us wait at the tomb,
> Quickened and raised together with Christ,
> Yet lingering still in its gloom;
> Some of us bide at the Passover feast
> With Pentecost all unknown,
> The triumphs of grace in the heavenly place
> That our Lord has made our own.[114]

As a teenager Annie aspired to be a concert pianist and composer, and she created melodies for some of her poems. But when arthritis slammed the lid on her musical dreams, Annie spent more time writing poetry, a talent that had first emerged when she was 9 years old. At first writing poetry was a replacement for her musical ambitions. Then "she ceased to regard her poems merely as a compensation for the loss of her music, and came to see in them the work and the ministry to which God was calling her from the beginning."[115] As she recalled God's leading in spite of her pain, she saw the divine call to use her poetic skills for spiritual purposes.

> *When we have exhausted*
> *our store of endurance,*
> *When our strength has failed*
> *ere the day is half done,*
> *When we reach the end*
> *of our hoarded resources,*
> *Our Father's full giving*
> *is only begun.**

Some Christian friends, concerned for her welfare, told Annie that Christ provided complete physical healing in the Atonement. They urged her to obey God and claim deliverance from her physical bondage. Annie

> listened to what they had to say. More than that, she went earnestly and prayerfully to search the Scriptures as to God's will. It was only after most painstaking study and prayer, and the reading of the best writers on this subject that she reached the conclusion that, while God can and does heal in this way in some cases, in others He does not; that He has seen fit to leave

some of the most triumphant saints deeply afflicted. . . . Miss Flint became thoroughly convinced that God intended to glorify Himself through her, in her weak, earthen vessel, and while like Paul she had three times, and more, prayed that this might be taken from her, there came to her with real assurance the voice which said, "My grace is sufficient for thee. My strength is made perfect in weakness."[116]

So she pushed the pen through her bent fingers, or used her knuckles to strike typewriter keys, and wrote in rhyme about her journey with God.

> *Shut in—shut in from the ceaseless din*
> *Of the restless world, and its want and sin.*
> *Shut in from its turmoil, care and strife*
> *And all the wearisome round of life.*
> *Shut in, with tears that are spent in vain.*
> *With the dull companionship of pain;*
> *Shut in with the changeless days and hours,*
> *And the bitter knowledge of failing powers.*
> *Shut in with a trio of angels sweet,*
> *Patience and Grace all pain to meet,*
> *With Faith that can suffer and stand and wait,*
> *And lean on the promises strong and great!*
> *Shut in with Christ! Oh, wonderful thought!*
> *Shut in with the peace His sufferings brought;*
> *Shut in with the love that wields the rod,*
> *Oh, company blest! Shut in with God!*[117]

Even when her own pain screamed for attention, Annie thought of others and their needs. This is evident in her poem "The Prayer in the Night."

> *Sometimes I wake with dark and quiet around me,*
> *And swift across my vision, like a light,*
> *Flashes the face of one I know who suffers,*
> *Or one whom sorrow newly touched last night.*
> *Perhaps, for just that moment and that purpose,*
> *There lacks a link in God's great chain of prayer;*
> *So, lest the chain be weakened by my silence,*
> *Or break because I fail to do my share,*
> *I shape the link, and know the Spirit's fire*
> *Will forge it into place and weld it there.*[118]

Annie's poems were printed on greeting cards, on wall hangings, and in magazines. Payment for the use of these poems never covered her increasing medical bills. In 1926 an article in *The Sunday*

School Times resulted in 3,000 people sending letters of encouragement and cash to Annie within seven weeks. *The Evangelical Christian* collected $1,000 from its readers for her.

Her popularity as a poet grew because her poems revealed the depth of her own experiences. People recognized themselves in her words. But more than that, she used the truth of God's Word like a pair of reading glasses through which to view her experiences. As a woman of faith, her eyes were always lifted above her own suffering to see the gracious Savior who provided comfort.

"He Giveth More Grace" (*Sing to the Lord* No. 101)

In 1933 Hubert Mitchell and his family were preparing to be missionaries to Sumatra, Indonesia. For several years Hubert and his wife had served as song evangelists, and he was leading music for a crusade in Minneapolis, Minnesota, shortly before going overseas. One day while praying, Hubert "saw this poem on the wall of the pastor's study. It intrigued me deeply, and, as I read it over and over again, the latter part of the chorus came singing into my mind, 'He giveth and giveth and giveth again.' I walked around the auditorium of the church singing the refrain, and then within about one-half hour, the whole verse and chorus came to me as from the Lord. I hastily wrote it down as I played it over several times on the piano."[119]

Hubert believed that this experience confirmed God's call for his missionary service. Even though he was taking his family to live in primitive conditions, God would provide everything they would need.

FOR FURTHER READING

Bingham, Rowland Victor. *The Life of Annie Johnson Flint.* Grand Rapids: Zondervan Publishing House, n.d.

Flint, Annie Johnson. *Annie Johnson Flint's Best Loved Poems.* Toronto: Evangelical Publishers, 1955.

Barney E. Warren
(1867-1951)

In the late 1880s, the evangelistic team that included Barney Warren traveled from Beaver Dam to Sweetser, Indiana. The group stopped at a grove of trees to eat lunch. Frances Miller, another member of the group, described the scene in her diary: "We spread our dinner upon Father's green carpet, then thought we would praise Him with a song. In a few moments we were surrounded with cattle. There must have been at least twenty-five or thirty, with their eyes wide open, gazing at us. We felt God had put the love of music in these dumb animals, and we sang two or three songs for their benefit."[120]

Always singing the sweet song of salvation—that describes the ministry of the evangelistic team formed by Daniel Warner. Whether riding in a wagon to hold a revival service, or standing before the congregation, "Warner's Band" was known for its fine singing.

In the 1870s, Warner had come under the influence of the Wesleyan/Holiness Movement. He formed the evangelistic team, Christian workers who also sang as a mixed quartet, to proclaim full salvation through an itinerant ministry. Out of their ministry the Church of God (Anderson) was born.

Andrew Byers remembered his parents hosting Warner's Band in 1888. He wrote, "During their stay in our home, Brother Warren did some composing at the organ, and this seemed wonderful to me. I had never seen such people, whose countenances were aglow with the victory of salvation and who were so filled with praise and song."[121]

Barney Warren traveled for five years with the Warner evangelistic team. No one was surprised when he left home while still a teenager to join this ministry. He was a talented singer, raised in a musical family that often formed a double quartet to sing Stephen Foster songs. His own conversion resulted from the ministry of an evangelistic team similar to the one he later joined.

Barney was converted after J. C. Fisher and a band of Christian workers held services near Bangor, Michigan. Their ministry brought revival to the region. One family touched by God during this revival was the Abbott family. Barney worked on their farm at the time. After the Fisher team left, home prayer meetings continued and many people were converted. Barney attended a prayer meeting in the Abbott home and was invited to seek the Lord, but Barney said he wasn't ready. The grace of God continued to woo him until at the second prayer meeting he attended, Barney was saved. "Bowing there in that farmhouse, consecrated by the godly lives of Father Abbott and his family and by the tears and prayers of those who gathered there to plead for the lost, Barney found Christ waiting for him. For the first time in his life he was sensible of the power of forgiving love. He rose from his knees, cleansed and happy."[122]

He pardoned my transgressions;
He sanctified my soul.
He honors my confessions
Since by His blood I'm whole.
It is truly wonderful
what the Lord has done!
Glory to His name!

The revival fires burned intensely in that region. Groups of singers and exhorters held meetings in neighboring communities. Sixteen-year-old Barney Warren was a leader in this effort. These meetings were still in progress a year later when Daniel Warner visited the area. Besides preaching services, Warner observed the ministry of the gifted Barney Warren. When Barney was 18, just two years after his conversion, he became the bass singer in Warner's Band.

Warner and Warren began collaborating, writing many gospel songs. Warner wrote the words; Warren composed the melody. Later Barney started writing both the words and the music for his songs. Barney eventually wrote about 7,000 songs.

When Barney left the Warner evangelistic team, he studied music harmony and hymnology at the Quincy (Illinois) Music School and Moody Bible Institute. Then he returned to the work of evangelism. He held several pastorates, but he always had the pioneer spirit. He would serve a congregation as its pastor, primarily doing the work of the evangelist, then turn the work over to a pastor/teacher. He would then go to another community to repeat the process.

Barney Warren's total commitment to the gospel was revealed in a revival series he conducted in Bedford, Indiana, in 1917. A small congregation had been started in this town but had never become firmly established. The faithful few asked Barney to hold revival meetings. Although the weather was cold, revival fires burned hot and many people presented themselves to the Lord in total consecration.

On the last Sunday of the meeting, Barney was trapped by a blizzard in a town 10 miles away from where the services were held. No one would rent him a horse. The train would not run since the steam was freezing in the boilers. Being a man of conviction and integrity, Barney believed he must be at the final revival meeting. So in spite of blizzard conditions, he walked along the train tracks for almost three hours to preach at the final meeting. These meetings were a turning point for this congregation. The example of Barney Warren, a committed Christian, made the difference in those lives.[123]

"It Is Truly Wonderful" (*Sing to the Lord* No. 381)

Barney Warren counseled a young woman who had responded to an altar call but was troubled by all that she would give up if she committed herself to the Lord. Brushing aside her list of dos and don'ts, Barney encouraged her to trust Christ for salvation, then to let God direct her decisions about those matters. She followed Barney's advice and was saved that day.

Several years later Barney met this woman again. She told him that all of the things she thought she'd miss were nothing compared with knowing Christ. Then she added, "I am fully satisfied in the service of the Lord—it is all so wonderful."[124] This phrase inspired Barney to write "It is truly wonderful what the Lord has done! Glory to His name!"

"Joy Unspeakable" (*Sing to the Lord* No. 423)

Barney Warren was working in a camp meeting in northwestern Ohio. Needing solitude, he left the campgrounds to find a quiet place where he could pray and meditate. His excursion took him past an artesian well. "The water was flowing with great force in a stream the full size of the pipe. I threw a chip into the pipe, but the force of the water was so great that it carried the chip away. I then picked up a large stick of wood about a foot in length and forced it down the pipe, but the powerful stream quickly brought it up and carried it away."[125]

Barney recalled Jesus' words to the woman at Jacob's well, "Whosoever drinketh of the water that I shall give him shall never thirst; but the water that I shall give him shall be in him a well of water springing up into everlasting life" (John 4:14, KJV). He thought of Peter's words, "Though now ye see him not, yet believing, ye rejoice with joy unspeakable and full of glory" (1 Pet. 1:8, KJV). While Barney looked at the artesian well and meditated on these scriptures, a song formed in his mind. He gave his own testimony when he wrote that the joy of Jesus was "like a great o'erflowing well springing up within my soul."

FOR FURTHER READING

Bolitho, Axchie A. *To the Chief Singer: A Brief Story of the Work and Influence of Barney E. Warren.* Anderson, Ind.: Gospel Trumpet Company, 1942.

M. Lorene Good
(1874-1962)

Paul Hansen knelt beside the bed in which his wife, Elizabeth, lay unconscious. She had given birth to their third child, Martha Lorene, on March 5, 1874. As the winter winds blew snow through the cracks between the logs in the cabin, Paul knew Elizabeth straddled the gulf separating this world from the next. No doctors were near to help these Nebraska pioneers—just a neighbor and their Heavenly Father.

God answered prayer. Both the mother and the baby girl survived. After she recovered, Elizabeth, or Lizzie as they called her, talked about her experience. She described Jesus standing at the foot of her bed calling for her amid a beautiful scene. But in her vision Lizzie remembered her children. She told Jesus that if she could remain on earth to raise her children, she would give her newborn to God for Christian service. God answered Lizzie's prayer, and Lizzie kept her promise.

Lorene, or Rena as family members referred to her, was never sturdy physically. She always worked inside the log house while her siblings did the harder chores outside. The family attended the Methodist church in Wood River, Nebraska, where Rena enjoyed the Sunday School library. She especially loved to read about the African adventures of Mary Moffat and David Livingstone.

Rena was a good student. After she won the county spelling contest, the school board asked her to teach. While still a teenager she earned a teaching certificate and started working in Hall County schools. She later graduated from the Normal School at Fremont, Nebraska, with a 96 percent average.

When Rena was 18 she started teaching the third graders at David City, Nebraska. One day the principal had her read an announcement to her students about children's services at a tent revival meeting. Rena felt she should attend the meeting to encourage her pupils. The next Sunday morning she walked to the grove where the organizers had pitched a large tent. As Rena entered the tent, she saw people lining the mourner's bench for a preservice prayer meeting. Rena joined them as they prayed for the services.

Rena returned that evening and sat at the back of the tent with a friend. Writing in the third person, Rena wrote:

> The power of God was on the service; not a word of the sermon did Miss Hansen hear, but a strong pull came on her as an altar call was given. . . . She found herself moving forward where she knelt at the mourner's bench; she hardly knew why. The meeting was dismissed and saints began to pray and sing, "I can and I will and I do believe" and before she knew it a light came into Miss Hansen's heart. She had always believed God hears prayer, now she knew it. She knew God as her own Father.[126]

A woman who was a singer with the evangelistic team walked home with Rena that evening. They talked about the Christian life. The singer told Rena she was the only convert at the 10-day meeting.

Sweeping this way, yes, sweeping this way,
A mighty revival is sweeping this way.
Keep on believing; trust and obey.
A mighty revival is sweeping this way.

Rena's faith was tested within a year when she was diagnosed with tuberculosis. One lung was closed, and the upper portion of the other was infected. Rena did not teach school that year.

By 1895 her health improved enough for her to consider teaching again. After attending revival meetings with a Quaker evangelist, Rena decided to give her life to mission work. Her skill as a teacher and her devotion to Christian service found mutual fulfillment as Rena taught 80 children for the World's Faith Missionary Association's Faith Mission at Shenandoah, Iowa.

Occasionally Rena's health would worsen, and the community would pray for her healing. Tired of physical limitations, Rena longed for complete healing. While lying at the base of a tree in Oak Park, Des Moines, Iowa, Rena asked God to heal her, pledging to then give her life for missionary service in India.

But instead of getting better, her condition worsened. The people of the World's Faith Missionary Association secretly planned her funeral. Her feet swelled, and she could not stand without great pain. One afternoon, in the quiet bedroom, Rena became aware of God's presence. She felt God touch her forehead, then withdraw. Her feet were still swollen.

The next morning two women checked on Rena and, thinking she was asleep, quietly closed the bedroom door. Again Rena sensed

God's presence. She heard Him instruct her to go to the morning prayer meeting. When she obeyed God by faith, she found that all pain had gone. Her feet were still swollen, so she squeezed them into an extra-large pair of shoes left for mission use and started the nine block trip to the meeting place. She arrived at the prayer meeting a half hour late and testified to God's healing touch. God healed her of tuberculosis that day.

Rena kept her promise to God. In April 1899 she left New York to go to India as a missionary. In 1905 Rena married Charles Good, an India-born man of British ancestry who was helping with famine relief. After seven years in India, Rena returned to her family in Nebraska because of her husband's poor health. When the Church of the Nazarene began in Grand Island, Nebraska, in 1913, Sister Good was a charter member. Throughout her life she was known as a woman who knew God intimately and was quick to testify to God's touch on her life.

"Sweeping This Way" (*Sing to the Lord* No. 718)

Sister Good loved camp meetings and revival services. This song showcases her enthusiasm. While she wrote many poems for church publications and the local newspaper, this is her only hymn.

The music for this hymn was first published in 1895 with the title "Looking This Way." Both the text and the tune of this song were written by Judson W. Van DeVenter, an evangelist and song writer. "Looking This Way" became quite popular.

We may never know how Lorene Good's text and Judson Van DeVenter's tune came to be joined. Given the popularity of "Looking This Way," Lorene Good may have written her poem with this tune in mind. Early editions of "Sweeping This Way" indicate that the tune was arranged by Haldor Lillenas. He may have placed Sister Good's poem with Van DeVenter's melody. This hymn has appeared in every official Church of the Nazarene hymnal.

Lorene Good's song "Sweeping This Way" was arranged by Haldor Lillenas. For more information on Lillenas, see pages 69-76.

FOR FURTHER READING

Good, Martha Lorene Hansen. "Sketches of the Past." Unpublished autobiography, n.d.

Haldor Lillenas
(1885-1959)

With $9 in his pocket, Haldor Lillenas boarded a Southern Pacific train in Portland, Oregon. His destination was Deets Pacific Bible College in Los Angeles.[127] Wanting to support this young man who felt God's call to Christian ministry, the people of Portland First Church of the Nazarene had purchased his train ticket. The pastor's wife, Mrs. A. O. Hendricks, had prepared enough food to last his whole trip.

When he arrived in Los Angeles, Haldor looked for a job that would allow him to work half-days while attending school—a daunting task in 1909. While walking from business to business asking the owners if they needed help, Haldor arrived on a deserted Los Angeles street. There, he was shocked to see a man beating a woman.

> There being no one else in the immediate vicinity to improve the situation, I felt it my duty to interfere in the unequal struggle. So, grasping the scoundrel firmly by the shoulder, I jerked him out of reach of the unfortunate lady, who proved to be his wife. He did not take kindly to my interference and came back at me with a more or less vigorous right to the jaw. I responded in like manner. I was not a trained boxer in any sense of the word, but he went down rather unceremoniously. . . . I was unable to play the piano for some weeks for obvious reasons.[128]

Haldor had seen the harsh side of city life before. Beginning in 1906 he ministered at city missions in Astoria and Portland, Oregon, and San Francisco and Santa Rosa, California. For a few months in 1908 he traveled with the Charioteers' Brigade, a musical group in the Salvation Army. In fact his own conversion had occurred at a city mission.

In 1886 Manie Payne Ferguson, author of the hymn "Blessed Quietness" (*Sing to the Lord* No. 313), and her husband, Theodore, founded Peniel Mission in Los Angeles. For a short while Phineas F. Bresee, founding general superintendent of the Church of the Nazarene, was associated with this mission. In the 1890s other Peniel Missions were founded in West Coast towns, including a mission in Astoria, Oregon.

One evening in July 1906, Haldor Lillenas walked down an Astoria street. On one street corner people sang gospel songs and testified about God's saving power. When the street meeting ended, "the lady in charge of the service announced a meeting to follow in the little Peniel Mission 'on Fifth Street just above Commercial.'"[129] Haldor followed the crowd into the unpretentious hall.

Haldor was initially attracted by a young woman's song on that street corner. The song spoke of a prodigal son who left home, leaving a grieving mother:

> She almost broke her loving heart in mourning after me;
> And day and night she prayed to God to keep me in His care.
> O angels, tell my mother I'll be there.

As the woman sang, Haldor recalled his own mother who had died of tuberculosis three years earlier. She had been a strong Christian who had provided spiritual training for her children.

While Haldor was growing up, the Lillenas family had devotions morning and evening. From when he was 4 years old until he was 14, his family lived on a homestead in the forest about 13 miles from Astoria. No churches were nearby, although a minister from town would occasionally hold services. Most of the time, however, neighbors gathered in a home on Sunday to sing hymns and pray. Then one man would read a sermon from a book. Lillenas recalled that "at times it was possible for me to be seated near enough the reader to be able to see the pages as they were turned. Each time he turned the page I fervently hoped to be able to see the end of the discourse."[130] They did not have a Sunday School, but each Sunday Haldor's father taught his family catechism and the Bible using a question-and-answer format.

Others may deny the Lord and live in sin, But the race that I have entered I must win. Thro' the pearly gates I mean to enter in. I have settled the question forever.

In 1900 the Lillenas family moved from Oregon to Minnesota. During that summer Haldor attended a Norwegian religious school. When he was 15 he was confirmed in the Lutheran church. In his autobiography Haldor wrote that his confirmation "was a most solemn day for me, as I knelt at the sacred altars of the country church with other members of my confirmation class and promised solemnly that I would forsake the world, the flesh, and the devil. This promise was made in all sincerity but I soon discovered, to my sorrow, that without the miracle of the new birth it was impossible to keep this pledge."[131]

Life was not the same in the Lillenas home after Haldor's mother died. Haldor decided to set out on his own. He worked on farms in Minnesota and grubbed stumps in the forest and fished the Pacific Ocean near Astoria. He returned to North Dakota to work on his father's farm. Once again he moved to Astoria, this time working in a box factory. Then he heard the song on the street corner. After 4 years of searching for his life's work, situations were about to change for Haldor.

Two weeks after he first heard the group singing on the streets, Haldor was converted at the Peniel Mission. "I found my way to an altar of prayer and in those few moments of earnest confession and supplication, at the little Peniel Mission, I became a new creature in Christ Jesus, old things had

The burden that once I carried is gone.
Of all of my sins there remaineth not one.
Jesus, the Savior, hath ransomed me,
Bearing my sins upon Calvary,
Giving me glorious liberty;
My burden of sin is gone.*

passed away, behold, all things had become new! Three months later, after many struggles, I sought and found the blessing of heart purity."[132]

He started assisting with the ministry of the Peniel Mission, working with the music, the street meetings, and with evangelism efforts.

Immediately after his conversion, Haldor started writing gospel songs. He had written secular songs before, but now his creative efforts were used for spiritual purposes. William Kirkpatrick sent him a letter of encouragement and published one of his early songs, "The Way He Leads Is Best for Me." Isaiah G. Martin, a Nazarene pastor and songbook compiler, published "He Set Me Free," a song that was widely used in camp meetings in the 1910s.

As Haldor's ministry involvement increased, he realized his need for further training. That's when he enrolled in Deets Pacific Bible College.

While at Deets Pacific, Haldor met and married Bertha Mae Wilson, a gifted singer, songwriter, and preacher. Haldor was in school just one year when the young couple began pastoral ministry.

---

*© 1923, Renewed 1951 by Lillenas Publishing Co.

From 1910 to 1926 they served congregations in California, Illinois, Texas, and Indiana. Between pastoral assignments—and sometimes in addition to pastoral responsibilities—Haldor participated in camp meetings and revival crusades. Many of his most enduring hymns were written and first used in evangelistic campaigns. In all, he composed nearly 4,000 songs.

In 1924 Haldor and others formed Lillenas Publishing Company to print gospel songbooks. The effort was successful, and in 1930 the Nazarene Publishing House purchased Lillenas Publishing Company as its music division. Haldor moved with the Lillenas Publishing Company from Indianapolis to Kansas City. One of his initial responsibilities in Kansas City was to produce the first official hymnal of the Church of the Nazarene, *Glorious Gospel Hymns*. He continued to manage the company that bore his name until his retirement in 1950.

After Haldor's death in 1959, his friend and colleague Floyd Hawkins wrote a poem of tribute titled "He Set the World to Singing." The second stanza read,

> *He met God at the altar where saving grace was found,*
> *And grace became his soul-possessing theme.*
> *So wonderful the blessing and grace did so abound*
> *That songs were born like one melodic stream.*[133]

"My Wonderful Lord" (*Sing to the Lord* No. 111)

One morning in 1938 as Haldor drove to the Nazarene Publishing House, he was facing a time of great personal difficulty.

> It was a gray day, chilly, with some fog and smoke in the air. Both of our children had married and left home. My wife was very ill, and it was with a heavy heart that I had left home that morning. I recalled brighter days, when we were busy in our much-loved pastorates and when we had the children at home. Now I was busy writing songs, compiling and editing books, doing what I felt God had called me to do; but I sometimes wondered how many of them would be sung. Suddenly as I drove along the avenue it seemed that Someone quietly opened the car door and sat down beside me. I could feel the warmth of His sacred presence and I began to sing quietly:
>
> > *My wonderful Lord, my wonderful Lord,*
> > *By angels and seraphs in heaven adored!*[134]

"Come Just As You Are" (*Sing to the Lord* No. 321)

In 1927 Haldor Lillenas attended a service at the Chicago Gospel

Tabernacle. Evangelist Paul Rader pled for people to seek the Lord. He said, "Do not wait to better your condition, do not endeavor to improve yourself, but come just as you are."[135] Haldor wrote this invitation hymn that night.

"Wonderful Grace of Jesus" (*Sing to the Lord* No. 360)

Haldor and Bertha Mae copastored the Church of the Nazarene in Auburn, Illinois, from 1916 to 1919. Sometimes Haldor would be away from home for several weeks while Bertha Mae continued the pastoral work. During one of these times, Haldor served as a song evangelist in Tallulah, Illinois. While in Tallulah he stayed with a blacksmith, a faithful member of the congregation, who worked in a shop next to his home. The revival meetings were held in the evenings, and during the days Haldor wrote songs. At this time he was writing songs for Charles Alexander, a song evangelist with a worldwide ministry. "Wonderful Grace of Jesus" was written in 1918 in Tallulah.

The song was designed for a choir but quickly became a congregational song. Lillenas deplored the fact that "most people sing it too fast. A song should be performed in such a fashion that the words can be comfortably pronounced without undue haste."[136]

As was typical in 1918, Haldor sold the song for $5 and received no royalties even though his creation was widely distributed. After he joined the music publishing business he had to pay as much as $50 for permission to use "Wonderful Grace of Jesus" in his compilations.

"Under the Atoning Blood" (*Sing to the Lord* No. 387)

In 1917 Haldor directed music at a revival in Joplin, Missouri. Many found the Lord, but Haldor felt the meetings lacked a freedom of spirit. People were preoccupied with the news of World War I. City noises constantly filled the air. Wickedness and corruption seemed to dominate city life. Haldor wrote,

> One day I felt my need of a season of secret prayer and so, using my church key, I entered the dimly lighted sanctuary. . . . A lovely upright piano had been made available for our use during the special services. I sat down to this instrument and began idly to finger the keys. Through the narrow slits of the tall, richly stained windows a crimson light spilled across the white ivories. Into my heart a song came singing:
>
> *I have found a precious resting place*
> *In the shelter of redeeming grace.*

Here with joy I see my Savior's face,
Under the atoning blood.

In that noisy, wicked city I had found a place of quiet and cleansing. . . . Like the spotless lily blooming amidst the grime and soot of a factory town, still snow-white and undefiled, so the soul of man can be kept spotless in a world of sin.[137]

"I Have Settled the Question" (*Sing to the Lord* No. 399)

Once in Auburn, Illinois, inclement weather prevented many people from attending a weekly prayer meeting. One woman who did go to the church testified, "No matter what others may do, I have settled the question that I am going through with the Lord." Haldor kept thinking about the testimony and in a few days both the words and the music were written.[138]

"Holiness Forevermore" (*Sing to the Lord* No. 502)

A few months after he arrived at Deets Pacific Bible College in Los Angeles, Haldor became the music director for a local congregation. He wrote this song for his church choir.

In the sermon delivered at the memorial service for Haldor Lillenas, Church of the Nazarene General Superintendent G. B. Williamson said that Lillenas's "songs are an expression of the inner life of holiness, devotion, communion, and joy. They are what they are because he was what he was, by the grace of God. They were an outpouring of his life for the joy of others and for the glory of God."[139]

"Wonderful Peace" (*Sing to the Lord* No. 591)

In 1914 Haldor was a member of an evangelistic team holding a crusade for 23 churches of several denominations in Pueblo, Colorado. The meetings were held in a 5,000-seat tabernacle erected for the occasion. Haldor not only helped with the music but also directed midday meetings held at various businesses. One night the evangelist, Dr. Charles Reign Scoville, spoke on "The Peace of God." This hymn was Haldor's response to the sermon.[140]

Dr. D. I. Vanderpool, general superintendent of the Church of the Nazarene, said that "Christ was always exalted in [Lillenas's] songs as the source of strength for the weak, comfort for the sorrowing, and deliverance for the enslaved."[141] The truth of that summary statement is evident in the final lines of this hymn,

Since my Redeemer has ransomed my soul
I have peace, sweet peace.

"Jesus Will Walk with Me" (*Sing to the Lord* No. 603)

While Haldor pastored the Church of the Nazarene in Redlands, California, a neighboring pastor asked his assistance with revival services. The piano player did well when she played for the congregational singing. However, she caused frustration when she accompanied Haldor for a vocal solo. "She was more or less inclined to substitute her own harmonies for the original chords."[142] Haldor did not complain but developed an alternative plan. "I decided I would play my old guitar as accompaniment to my special numbers and that, since I was not a very proficient guitarist, I would write a few songs that would be simple enough to be sung with the simple chords which were at my command."[143]

"Jesus Will Walk with Me" was one of the songs written for that revival series.

"Where They Need No Sun" (*Sing to the Lord* No. 654)

Haldor wrote this song while he pastored in Lompoc, California. "One Sunday evening while the sun, like a golden disk, lost itself in a violet cloud bank,"[144] Haldor finished his sermon for the Sunday evening service. He was reading Rev. 21:23, "And the city had no need of the sun, neither of the moon, to shine in it: for the glory of God did lighten it, and the Lamb is the light thereof." As he meditated on this verse and watched the sunset, he thought "the city where they need no sun" would be a suitable theme for a gospel song. After the service that evening he wrote the words. The next morning he set the text to music.

Haldor Lillenas was a mentor to Floyd Hawkins. For more information on Hawkins, see pages 75-81.

OTHER HYMNS BY HALDOR LILLENAS

"Don't Turn Him Away" (*Sing to the Lord* No. 333)
"Wonderful" (*Sing to the Lord* No. 377)
"My Burden Is Gone" (*Sing to the Lord* No. 405)
"Glorious Freedom" (*Sing to the Lord* No. 505)
"The Closer I Walk" (*Sing to the Lord* No. 599)
"It Is Glory Just to Walk with Him" (*Sing to the Lord* No. 610)
"A Closer Walk with Thee" (*Sing to the Lord* No. 617)
"Tell the Blessed Story" (*Sing to the Lord* No. 695)

FOR FURTHER READING

Cunningham, Elaine. *Haldor Lillenas: The Marvelous Music Maker.* Kansas City: Beacon Hill Press of Kansas City, 1992.

Lillenas, Haldor. *Down Melody Lane.* Kansas City: Lillenas Publishing Company, 1953.

———. *Modern Gospel Song Stories.* Kansas City: Lillenas Publishing Company, 1952.

McGraw, James. "The Preaching of Haldor Lillenas," *Preacher's Magazine,* 36 (May 1961), 5-8.

Ramquist, Grace. *The Boy with the Singing Heart.* Kansas City: Beacon Hill Press, 1960.

Temple, Helen F. "Music Man of Melody Lane." *Holiness Digest* 4 (Fall 1990), 7-9.

White, Stephen S. "Sky-born Music." *Herald of Holiness* 48 (September 30, 1959), 12-13.

———, ed. "Dr. Haldor Lillenas." *Herald of Holiness* 48 (September 30, 1959), 14-16.

Young, Bill. *A Song Is Born: The Story of Haldor Lillenas.* Kansas City: Beacon Hill Press of Kansas City, 1978.

Floyd W. Hawkins
(1904-)

"Heeeeere's Johnny."

As Floyd Hawkins watched Johnny Carson perform *The Tonight Show* monologue one evening, he didn't anticipate that the inspiration for a song was just minutes away. During his songwriting career many things had kindled the creative fire: a mountain stream, a biblical story, an economic depression, a spiritual victory. But this was the first time a secular television broadcast prompted Floyd's creation of a gospel song.

That evening Johnny Carson interviewed Carl Sagan, popular science speaker and writer. As Floyd listened to Sagan describe the universe, two things caught his attention: the immensity of the universe and scientists' broad degree of understanding. The creative juices started flowing, as they often did late at night for Floyd, and he began to write.

> The wisdom of this world is so amazing,
> As men survey the earth and distant space;
> But there's a realm that's far beyond all measure,
> The fathomless expanse of God's great grace.*

And the song "God's Great Grace" was born.[145]

Floyd grew up in a home filled with music. Even before he was born both his father, a baritone, and his mother, an alto, sang in the choir of their Methodist church in Foster, Missouri. After the birth of their first child, the Hawkins family moved west by rail, settling in the state of Washington. Becoming established in a new town included joining the local Methodist church and singing in its choir.

On November 20, 1904, Floyd Wesley Hawkins was born in Pullman, Washington. A year later the family moved 80 miles to Walla Walla, Washington, so Sam Hawkins could better support his family—which eventually included six children. This move provided an environment in which Floyd flourished musically. This relatively small town in an agricultural region provided rich cultural re-

---

sources. Music lessons were readily available. Some of the finest musicians in the world presented concerts in Walla Walla.

Floyd took full advantage of the musical opportunities. He enrolled in every music class the high school offered—band, orchestra, glee club, and a sight-singing class. He played trumpet in several brass ensembles that performed at civic and social functions in the city. Floyd organized and directed a pep band that traveled with the high school football team. Sundays were especially full of music.

> On Sunday mornings at 9 o'clock I was at the First Presbyterian Church rehearsing with Brunton's Orchestra, an orchestra that for many years played for social events throughout the city. Following rehearsal we would remain and play for their Sunday School as payment for the use of their facilities. From there I would walk up to the First Nazarene Church and play for the morning worship service. At night I played with the orchestra at White Temple Baptist Church.[146]

When the Church of the Nazarene started a congregation in Walla Walla, the Hawkins family soon transferred their membership. In their new church Floyd experienced joyful, exuberant singing. He and his friends responded to altar calls at nearly every revival meeting the church held, but real spiritual establishment came as Floyd entered adulthood.

Even though Floyd had graduated from high school and was old enough to be on his own, he moved with the family to Tacoma, Washington, when his father found better employment. The pastor of the Nazarene church in Tacoma, Rev. V. W. Anglin, took a special interest in Floyd, inviting him on pastoral errands. This relationship cultivated the soil for the gospel to bud.

On Easter Sunday evening in 1926, Floyd attended the final service of a two-week revival series led by evangelist Fred St. Clair. This became the moment of spiritual decision that determined the course Floyd would follow.

> The invitation hymn was being sung and although I was not greatly moved—having been through countless revival meetings in the old home church and having gone forward many times and making professions without understanding the true meaning of repentance and faith. As I stood there with strong resistance, I seemed to hear an inner voice saying, "Floyd, you are a fool if you don't go tonight."
>
> Without emotion I walked down the aisle and knelt at the altar. I tried to pray but it seemed to have no meaning. Others came and left, but I stayed, with one strong determination—

that I would not make a profession without being sure of something real. This "hang-up" was caused by my lack of understanding of the simplicity of faith. Perhaps I was expecting some kind of physical feeling or manifestation. I had confessed my sins many times in the past, only to meet with disappointment.

That night, at a very late hour, the truth dawned upon me. I stood up and, without a spark of feeling or emotion, testified that, on the authority of God's word (1 John 1:9), "I believe that I am saved." It was then that the light of truth fully broke upon me and for the first time in my life, I knew beyond a shadow of a doubt that my sins were forgiven. I was so happy that I spent a long time rejoicing.[147]

His spiritual conversion not only changed Floyd's heart but also transformed him as a musician. He began writing gospel songs to express his faith. Neighboring churches and camp meetings asked Floyd to help them with music for their evangelistic crusades. At one of these meetings, Floyd received a telegram from the district superintendent, informing him that he had been appointed as the pastor of the Church of the Nazarene in Hoquiam, Washington. The course of his life had been set.

> *O I have found it*
> *—the Crystal Fountain,*
> *Where all my life's*
> *deep needs have been supplied;*
> *So freely flowing*
> *from Calv'ry's mountain,*
> *And now my soul*
> *is fully satisfied.**

Floyd and his young bride, Ruth, served the Hoquiam congregation for just a few months before they launched a five-year journey as evangelists with the Parks-Hawkins Quartet. (The Parkses were Ruth's parents.) When they were expecting their first child, Floyd and Ruth returned to pastoral ministry, first in Medford and Parkdale, Oregon, then in Dinuba and Stockton, California. Floyd spent nearly 20 years in pastoral ministry, all the time refining his craft as a songwriter and musician. While he pastored the Stockton congregation he completed music studies at the University of the Pacific. In 1957 Floyd became the music editor at Lillenas Publishing Company, a position he held for 18 years. His responsibilities included editing the *Worship in Song* hymnal.

Floyd Hawkins published more than 500 songs. Some of them, such as "I've Discovered the Way of Gladness," have been sung around the world—in churches, at Billy Graham crusades, and on television programs. The young man converted in Tacoma, Washington, became a minister with a worldwide congregation through the songs he wrote.

"Let Thy Mantle Fall on Me" (*Sing to the Lord* No. 293)

Floyd Hawkins kept a "scrap file" in which he placed ideas for songs. When inspired by a thought, he'd find the first available piece of paper and jot down a phrase or a stanza, then drop it in the file for further consideration on another day. In 1962 Floyd found a piece of gray paper about four inches square on which he had written a chorus inspired by 2 Kings 2:9. Floyd didn't remember when he'd dropped that paper into the file, but the song that had long lay covered pushed through the fertile soil of his mind and began to blossom.

Soon after the song was written, Floyd attended a camp meeting at which Paul McNutt was the song evangelist. Paul asked Floyd if he had written any songs recently. Floyd told Paul about "Let Thy Mantle Fall on Me" and sent him a copy of the manuscript.

Paul used the new song in his next camp meeting at West Virginia. The people and evangelists responded enthusiastically. News of the song quickly spread, and people in other parts of the country started singing it. This occurred before Lillenas Publishing Company released a typeset printing of the song. Floyd Hawkins stated that no other song he wrote gained popularity as quickly as "Let Thy Mantle Fall on Me."[148]

"The Crystal Fountain" (*Sing to the Lord* No. 382)

They called it "God's Country." Located at the base of Mount Hood, the natural beauty of Parkdale, Oregon, and the wholesome life of the community made the Hawkinses' ministry there three years of pure joy. They often remembered those days with great fondness.

The memory of his experiences on Mount Hood inspired a new song while Floyd was pastoring the Church of the Nazarene in Stockton, California.

> In the spring, when the snow at lower elevations had melted, we would drive up the winding mountain slopes to Cloudcap Inn near the timberline. Then, by taking a trail up Cooper Spur, it was not far to a vantage point of unbelievable beauty overlooking Elliot Glacier. Beside the trail were many varieties

of wild flowers and everything spoke of freshness. Little streams and rivulets from snow-melt at higher elevations hurried down the mountainside. They were so crystal clear that at any point one could lie face-down and drink with full satisfaction, unquestioning its purity.[149]

This picture of God's creation became the catalyst for a song about God's re-creation of a human soul.

"Thou Wilt Keep Him in Perfect Peace" (*Sing to the Lord* No. 583)

While perusing songs for a publication project in 1960, Floyd noticed a chorus by Vivian A. Kretz. He had known the chorus for years but suddenly realized it might have a new life if expanded. As he studied the chorus it seemed the first half could be a stanza and the second half a refrain. Floyd wrote two more stanzas for the song and prepared the arrangement used today.

Twenty years before **Floyd Hawkins** became the music editor at Lillenas Publishing Company, Haldor Lillenas encouraged him to prepare for the job. For more information on Lillenas, see pages 69-76.

FOR FURTHER READING

Hawkins, Floyd W. "A Song Is Born." *Herald of Holiness* 43 (March 10, 1954): 27.
———. *The Way of Gladness.* Self-published, 1996.

George Beverly Shea
(1909-)

Bev awakened to the familiar sound of his mother's voice. In the days before clock radios he was always nudged to consciousness by her singing. Each weekday morning she played a brief introduction on the piano, then sang the refrain of the Eliza Hewitt/William Kirkpatrick song "Singing I Go" (*Sing to the Lord* No. 430).

> *Singing I go along life's road,*
> *Praising the Lord, praising the Lord,*
> *Singing I go along life's road,*
> *For Jesus has lifted my load.*

Neither Bev nor his mother could have predicted that 30 years later "Singing I Go" would be the theme song of his own radio show. While working at WMBI, the radio station associated with Moody Bible Institute in Chicago, Bev sang on a 15-minute radio program called "Hymns from the Chapel." He opened each morning's program by singing the song his mother used to awaken the Shea family.[150]

Bev's mother did more than just awaken him from sleep; she also aroused his interest in music. As a young boy Bev missed school most of his third and fourth grade years because of a lingering throat infection. His mother taught him, working with him at the kitchen table. She often asked Bev to read aloud while she prepared a meal. He read biblical passages and poems and hymns. Bev recalled: "Sometimes, moved by a particular hymn, Mother would take me into the living room, where our Bell piano sat, and play and sing the song to me. Then she would ask me to try it. Though I was no child prodigy, I could hack my way through a song at a fairly early age and because of her coaching and compliments, I kept practicing—and improving."[151]

Music often filled the Shea home. Bev's father would gather the family around the piano to sing. "The Bell piano was second only to the kitchen table as a family gathering place."[152] In addition to singing and playing the piano and organ, Bev played the violin.

Fred and Kitty Suffield were special friends of the Shea family.

They were like a favorite uncle and aunt to Bev. Fred was converted through the ministry of Bev's father, a Wesleyan Methodist pastor. Fred became an evangelist with the Church of the Nazarene. Rev. Shea often invited the Suffields to conduct revival services in his church. Sometimes when the Suffields were in the area, they asked Bev to help them with revival services.

One year Bev spent the month of August with the Suffields at a Methodist camp meeting in Ontario. During this tent meeting Bev played a violin solo and sang a solo for the first time in public. This was not a good experience for the 17-year-old boy. Standing outside of the tent, Bev was not aware that the congregation watched his silhouette as he combed his hair, trying to tame a stubborn cowlick. When he stepped into the tent to sing he was greeted with laughter by the crowd who had watched the show. Then his voice cracked during a high note. Bev didn't sleep that night. The next morning at breakfast he announced to the Suffields that he had sung his first and last solo. Kitty would not accept his declaration, however, and before the day was over they were practicing for his next solo, this time in a lower key.[153]

Bev confessed that at this time he was not a Christian. Although everyone in his family was saved, Bev knew about Jesus, but he did not know Christ as his personal Savior.

A year later, when he was 18, the Suffields held a two-week revival at Rev. Shea's church. Bev wrote:

> It was at these meetings that I really came under conviction for the first time. Every night when the altar call was given, I stood with the congregation and sang the invitational hymn with such gusto that the emotion which had built up inside me like a pressure cooker was released and the trip to the front was postponed again.
>
> My sensitive Dad knew a great war was being waged, but he never pushed me. As far as he was concerned, the decision was a matter between God and me.
>
> The services came down to the final night with me occupying a favorite seat in the very last row. Dad was on the platform with Fred Suffield.
>
> When Fred finished his sermon, he invited those who wanted to follow Christ to come forward. We began singing:
>> *Just as I am without one plea*
>> *But that Thy blood was shed for me*
>> *And that Thou bidd'st me come to Thee,*
>> *O Lamb of God, I come! I come!*

As we sang, Dad slipped down the side aisle and around in back of me. He put his hand on my shoulder and said: "Son, do you think tonight might be the night?"

"Yes, I do," I answered, and together we walked forward.[154]

"I'd Rather Have Jesus" (*Sing to the Lord* No. 456)

When Bev's father became the pastor of a Wesleyan congregation in Jersey City, New Jersey, 21-year-old Bev started working for the Mutual of New York Life Insurance Company in Manhattan. He began taking voice lessons from teachers in New York City and won $15 in a talent contest that was part of the Fred Allen radio program broadcast on NBC. Bev began to dream about a career as a professional singer.

Bev's mother realized her son was debating how he might use his musical talent. As she had done many times for all members of the Shea family, she left a slip of paper on the piano for Bev to discover. She had written the text from a song by Rhea Miller.

Rhea Miller, the daughter of a city mission worker, had accepted Jesus as her Savior when she was 18 years old. Attempting to disciple Rhea a few months after her conversion, her father suggested she write a song titled "I'd Rather Have Jesus." Eventually Rhea wrote the song in which she expressed her personal testimony.

The song remained on Rhea's shelf until her marriage. Then her husband, Rev. Howard Miller,[155] encouraged her to publish the song. About seven years after it was first published, Bev's mother placed a copy on the Shea piano.

Concerning the note his mother left on their piano, Bev wrote:

> Instead of practicing the hymn I had intended to play that Sunday morning in church, I turned to this poem. Melody just seemed to form around the words. When I had played and sung it through for the first time, Mother came from the kitchen where she had overheard. She wrapped both arms around my shoulders and placed her wet cheek next to mine.
>
> In church that morning, I sang for the first time, "I'd Rather Have Jesus."[156]

This song, the first that George Beverly Shea ever wrote, became his trademark. While living in New York he sang it in churches and Bible conferences. When he moved to Chicago he sang it on radio programs. In Chicago he met a young preacher named Billy Graham and eventually became a founding member of the Billy Graham crusade team. In this capacity he has sung "I'd Rather Have Jesus" in scores of countries around the world.

"The Wonder of It All" (*Sing to the Lord* No. 79)

In 1955 Bev was a passenger on the S.S. *United States* en route to Scotland for evangelistic meetings. During a conversation with another passenger, he was asked to describe a typical Billy Graham crusade. Bev wrote: "I found myself at a loss for words when I tried to describe the response that usually accompanied Mr. Graham's invitation to become a Christian. 'What happens then never becomes commonplace . . . watching people by the hundreds come forward . . . oh, if you could just see the wonder of it all.'"[157]

Unable to sleep that night, Bev kept thinking about the conversation. At 2 A.M. he got out of bed and wrote "The Wonder of It All" on the back of a ship's laundry list.

FOR FURTHER READING

Reese, Ed. *The Life and Ministry of Bev Shea.* Glenwood, Ill.: Fundamental Publishers, 1975.

Shea, George Beverly, and Fred Bauer. *Songs That Lift the Heart.* Old Tappan, N.J.: F. H. Revell, 1972.

———. *Then Sings My Soul.* Old Tappan, N.J.: F. H. Revell, 1968.

Walker, Robert. "Soft Music from a Warm Heart." *Christian Life* 47 (November 1985): 32-34, 36.

Byron M. Carmony
(1916-)

The country doctor entered the southern Indiana farmhouse to examine four-year-old Byron Carmony. The doctor saw a red streak of infection just beneath the skin's surface on one of the boy's legs. In the darkened bedroom the doctor lit a match and held it to the boy's eyes to check their reaction. Following his examination the doctor spoke with the boy's parents in hushed tones. "Meningitis. Inflammation of the brain tissue. . . . I don't think he'll live. . . . If he does there is a strong possibility that brain damage will limit normal development. . . . I'm sorry."

Being people of faith, the Carmony family would not give the doctor the final word concerning their young son. They called for family members and friends to come to their home to pray for healing. They gathered around Byron's bed, gently touching his infected body, and fervently asking God to be the Great Physician for this sick boy. God answered prayer. Byron gradually regained strength.

The faith in this experience exemplified the Carmony family's typical response to life's challenges. The Carmonys raised their nine children, six boys and three girls, in the church. The congregation knew that the Carmony family would attend every service. The faithfulness of his parents in their own spiritual pilgrimages and the training he received through the church taught Byron what it meant to be a Christian. His life illustrates the blessings that come to the person who trusts and obeys.

Byron wrote his first song, "On the Way to Glory," when he was seven years old. The song wasn't particularly innovative—many phrases were borrowed from testimonies he had heard at church services and cottage prayer meetings. Byron stated:

It's a little bit difficult for me to remember the details, but with that particular song I know I wrote it on a Sunday afternoon. In those days my dad would take a Sunday afternoon nap. While he was sleeping I wrote the song in three stanzas. I wrote it the way songs appear in a songbook. I wrote the first line of the first stanza and followed it with the first line of the second stanza, then the first line of the third stanza. So when I woke up Dad to tell him that I'd written a song, he read the lines in the order they were on the page. He said, "You have some good ideas, but they don't rhyme." I was a little provoked at him because I thought I was doing it pretty well. I was doing it like it was in the hymnal.[158]

When the Church of the Nazarene formed a congregation in Morristown, Indiana, Byron's parents were charter members. In March 1930 the congregation held revival meetings with evangelist H. N. Dickerson. Winter weather lingered during the week of revival and adversely affected attendance. But, as usual, the Carmony family attended faithfully. Byron was the only seeker at that revival series. He wrote, "I do not remember the sermon theme or invitation song. I do remember I knelt about three feet from the south end of the altar railing. I was very aware that at that service 'Jesus took my burden and left me with a song.' Something happened—guilt was gone and everything was made new."[159]

Byron naturally started serving his Savior in the church he attended. At 17 he became the Sunday School superintendent, but his primary avenue of service involved his natural musical ability. He taught

Then I met Jesus, wonderful Friend!
He loved and saved me, love without end.
Now I am walking close by His side.
*Storms may surround me; in Him I hide.**

himself to competently play the piano. Whenever a soloist needed a song transposed, Byron was asked to play the piano since he could easily play songs in any key.

When Byron arrived at Olivet Nazarene College in 1935 two grand pianos sat in the college chapel. The most proficient pianist would play "first" and another pianist would play "second." College officials asked Byron to play first piano during the chapel services, even though he had never taken a piano lesson. In fact, Byron couldn't read music until after he started piano lessons as a college junior. During his student years Byron wrote "Alma Mater, Olivet," which is still sung by students and alumni. Byron graduated from Olivet in 1941 with a bachelor of theology degree and a bachelor of arts degree with a teacher's certificate in music theory. Olivet honored him with a doctor of divinity degree in 1975.

---

*© 1936, Renewed 1964 by Lillenas Publishing Co. All rights reserved.

In spite of his extensive involvement in music, Byron believed God had called him to pastoral ministry. Some people urged him to pursue a career in music instead. Byron stated: "I remember one time when I was singing in a camp meeting, a tent meeting, and a Methodist preacher and his wife came to the services. I was just a teenager at the time and she asked me what I was going to do and I said that I was going to be a minister. She said, 'Oh, don't do that. Anybody can preach. You've got a gift of music and you need to emphasize that. You need to give your life to music.'"[160]

In 1941, when Byron and his wife, Virginia, moved to Harrisburg, Illinois, Byron wondered if he really could do the work of a minister. As he prepared to deliver his first sermon as the pastor of the Church of the Nazarene in Harrisburg, he painfully realized he had preached only once before.

A woman in the church didn't help his confidence. Byron had visited the Harrisburg church as a member of a quartet from Olivet. The quartet sold copies of Byron's song "Then I Met Jesus" to raise expense money. A picture of the quartet was printed with the music. Byron recalled, "In the first service as the pastor of the Harrisburg church, a woman said to me (with the quartet's picture in mind), 'Well, you're not the one we expected, but you'll be all right.'"[161]

As Byron began pastoring, God confirmed that he lived in the center of His will. He discovered that God utilized him to help people with eternal issues. For example, God used Byron in miraculous healing on two occasions. Byron said: "In my first pastorate the lady across the street from the parsonage had an almost continual flow of blood from an opening in a vein in her foot. She wanted me to pray for her. I prayed, like I always did, and the bleeding stopped and it didn't start up again. That was the end of it. She took that as instant healing. Right before my eyes. It was amazing."[162]

Another time a group of people prayed for a woman who was bedridden with a serious illness. "Everybody thought she was going to die. We anointed her and prayed. She got up out of her bed in her nightgown and shouted all over the house. That was the end of her sickness, and she lived several years after that."[163]

Byron spent 5 years in Harrisburg, then 22 years as the pastor of the Chicago Heights Church of the Nazarene, and 10 years in Elgin, Illinois. He continued writing songs, including the widely sung "He Became Poor" from the cantata *Mine Is a Risen Savior*. Based on the number of copies sold, Byron estimated that in one year about a thousand choirs used *Mine Is a Risen Savior*. He stated, "Since this cantata ended in an invitation song—and I did receive letters about a number of times when people came to the altar and were convert-ed—I felt like it was an extension of my ministry. It was a thrilling experience just to know that something I had done was being used beyond what I could see and hear."[164]

The faith exhibited by his parents when young Byron lay death-ly ill in an Indiana farmhouse was the same faith by which he lived his life. As he approached his 80th birthday he said, "Doing the will of God has never been a problem for me. Finding the will of God has been the real challenge. Life is easy once you know the will of God. After all, you decide that in your consecration, in the crisis ex-perience of the Holy Spirit coming in to rule your life."[165]

"Then I Met Jesus" (*Sing to the Lord* No. 356)

Byron met Jesus as his personal Savior and Lord in March 1930 when he was 13 years old. About two weeks after his conversion he sat at the piano improvising the melody and harmony that became "Then I Met Jesus." As he repeatedly played his new tune, words came to mind. Once the text started forming in his mind, he quickly completed the song. Byron recalled, "Since I did not know how to write the harmony, I had to get my high school music teacher to put it on paper."[166]

Byron sent the song to Haldor Lillenas for possible publication, but it was rejected. So Byron's father paid to have a song sheet print-ed. Within 10 years of this self-publication Lillenas wrote Byron ask-ing if he would sell the song to Lillenas Publishing Company, which he did. Byron wrote, "So far as I know, he [Lillenas] never realized it was the same song he had turned down years before."[167]

Byron first heard "Then I Met Jesus" sung by others at a district assembly. His quartet from Olivet had been asked to sing at the as-sembly. As the quartet entered the sanctuary, the song evangelists were singing "Then I Met Jesus" as a duet. God used that moment as a time of divine confirmation for Byron. In light of that experi-ence, he said, "I felt grateful. I felt like my life had a purpose. God was using me."[168] Tears came to Byron's eyes as he basked in the glow of God's approval.

David Livingstone Ives
(1921-87)

R. Wingrove Ives listened as the audience at the 1915 Apostolic Holiness Church Camp Meeting at Milton, Pennsylvania, sang "Keep On the Firing Line." He was the song leader and soloist for the camp meeting, but it was the congregation that ministered to Wingrove that day. Their spiritual fervor impressed him so much that Wingrove decided to join the Apostolic Holiness Church.[169]

Wingrove was born at Newcastle-on-Tyne, England, in 1893. Soon after his conversion in 1910, Wingrove began ministering as a gospel singer and preacher. The Wesleyan Methodist Church of England granted Wingrove a preacher's license. In 1913 he left England to attend Moody Bible Institute. After joining the Apostolic Holiness Church in 1915, he was ordained in 1916. He married Mary Catherine Kalbach in 1917.

That same year, again at the annual camp meeting at Milton, Wingrove and Mary heard God's call to preach the gospel among the people of the Caribbean islands. The Ives offered themselves to the church to serve as missionaries, and on December 31, 1919, along with their young son, John Wesley, they left New York harbor for Barbados.[170]

On June 5, 1921, this missionary couple rejoiced at the birth of their second son, David Livingstone, named after the missionary explorer. A daughter, Catherine Booth, joined the family in 1922. Both David and Catherine were born in Barbados and were British citizens at birth.

David's musical interest emerged early as he responded to the songs sung to him by the Barbados woman who cared for him. As David and the other Ives children grew, the family would gather around their piano to sing favorite songs and hymns. Dad had a rich baritone voice; Mom sang alto. The children sang melody.

Life was good for the Ives family in those days. David and Catherine were especially close, not only in age, but also as friends. The Ives home was filled with laughter and teasing, but David always defended his sister if someone else tried to tease her.

While he was a child in this loving Christian environment, David accepted Jesus as his Savior. The Iveses taught their children the spiritual disciplines, including daily Bible reading and prayer. David's mother urged him to read at least one chapter from the Bible each day. In typical fashion for a young boy, David often read from the Psalms because the chapters were shorter than those in other books of the Bible. In doing so, however, David began to understand God's design for music in worship.

The Ives family returned to the United States in 1932 for a furlough. During this time, 13-year-old David wrote his first sacred song, "He's the Best Friend." In January 1935 the Ives family returned to the Caribbean, this time going to Antigua. David's interest in music was nurtured at his school in Antigua, and he was always fascinated when he heard the organist play in the Moravian church there.

Because of unrest in the world, the Ives family came home again in 1937. David finished high school in Reading, Pennsylvania, where he was active in the glee club, the school chorus, and various quartets. During this time David and his brother operated a small printing press in their home, printing tracts and booklets for local customers. This experience would be useful later when David founded a music publishing company.

From the cross of Calvary
Shineth the Light of Life so free.
Sinner, "Look and live," saith He;
*Pardon is offered to thee.**

David's father traveled a great deal. While they lived in the Caribbean Wingrove was the field superintendent and would often be away visiting the congregations. When the family was in the United States, he would travel from city to city holding deputation services. During David's high school days a Christian businessman, Ward Printz, befriended David. Ward wrote gospel songs and was a fine singer and pianist. David spent hours talking with him about music. This mentor relationship was very important to David.

After his high school graduation, David attended Fort Wayne Bible Institute in Fort Wayne, Indiana, and Goshen College, in Goshen, Indiana. Through these years David continued to write gospel songs. When he completed his college education, David started his own music publishing company in Archbold, Ohio. Ives Music Press published many books of gospel songs, not only for

*© 1943, Renewed 1971 by Lillenas Publishing Co. All rights reserved.

congregational singing, but also for choirs, men's quartets, and women's trios. David organized a studio where he set the type for his music books.

In addition to his work as a publisher, David directed the music in a local church. He joined three other Christian businessmen to form a men's quartet, the Gospel Messengers, which sang for local churches. David sang bass.

David lived for Christ in every situation. His sister wrote, "I saw him live a consistent life, and he always had a tender heart. He was well loved by his neighbors and family, and everyone knew his stand for the Lord."[171] The solid spiritual foundation that was established early in his life produced spiritual fruit that brought honor to his Savior and Lord.

"On the Cross of Calvary" (*Sing to the Lord* No. 219)

One day David's fellow student at Fort Wayne Bible Institute, Richard Gerig, was practicing the organ in his home church when David entered the church. He listened to Richard play a tune he had written. David commented that the first phrase of the melody seemed to say "On the cross of Calvary."[172] That evening David wrote the first stanza and included it in his book *Inspirational Choruses* (1943). Four years later, while Richard and David were working on a book for men's quartets, David wrote stanza 2.

Richard Gerig was drafted soon after "On the Cross of Calvary" was written and served in the army during World War II. After his discharge, Richard completed his degree in music at Wheaton College. He worked in Christian radio at the Fort Wayne Bible College in the 1950s, also becoming the school's public relations director. In 1958 he returned to Wheaton College, serving in public relations for 30 years. Richard maintained his involvement in church music, serving as the music director for a local congregation, composing and arranging songs published by Lillenas Publishing Company and Hope Publishing Company, and serving on the editorial committee for a hymnal.

The creative life of David Livingstone Ives was cut short. While he was still in his 30s David was diagnosed with schizophrenia. In those days the disorder was not understood and treatments were minimal, so David was hospitalized for the last 30 years of his life. He tried to write songs after he became ill but was never again able to do so successfully. After David's hospitalization, the Lillenas Publishing Company acquired his publishing company and all copyrights, including "On the Cross of Calvary" and "I Want to Be Like Jesus."

In 1945 David Livingstone Ives wrote a melody for a text he adapted, titled "Perfect Trust." The poem is a source of comfort for a person of faith, like David Livingstone Ives, who faces difficult circumstances.

> *I may not always know the way*
> *Wherein God leads my feet;*
> *But this I know, that 'round my path*
> *His love and wisdom meet.*
>
> *I may not always understand*
> *Just why He sends to me*
> *Some bitter grief, some heavy loss;*
> *I'll trust though I can't see.*
>
> *My cherished plans and hopes may fail,*
> *My idols turn to dust,*
> *But this I know, my Father's love*
> *Is always safe to trust.*
>
> *Oh, precious peace within my heart;*
> *Oh, blessed rest to know*
> *A Father's love keeps constant watch,*
> *Amid life's ebb and flow.*

David Ives was delighted with Thomas Chisholm's response to his musical setting of Chisholm's hymn "I Want to Be Like Jesus" (*Sing to the Lord* No. 208). For more information on Chisholm and this hymn, see pages 54-57.

FOR FURTHER READING

Shafer, Ovella Satre. "David Livingstone Ives." *Conquest* 11 (December 1956): 43-44.
Thomson, Hazel. "Harvest of Songs." *Christian Etude* [8] (January 1954): 12.

Otis Skillings
(1935-)

In 1969 Otis Skillings entered the office of the Lillenas Publishing Company with a youth musical in his briefcase. He was excited about *Life*, a declaration of the abundant life offered by Jesus Christ set in a current, popular musical style. Skillings recalled, "I could sense that everyone was a little bit nervous. We were pushing the edges just a little bit. I sat down at the piano and played and sang *Life* just as though I were the choir."[173]

Lillenas Publishing Company's decision to release *Life* not only broke new ground for the company but also propelled youth ministry into new territory. Many churches formed youth groups for the first time. Existing youth groups were strengthened as this new tool became a catalyst for new ministries. With new music and new choreography and new outfits, teen choirs started singing *Life* at shopping centers, fairs, and prisons. Otis remembers with a chuckle that a teen choir from San Francisco sang *Life* at the San Quentin Prison, including a phrase from the theme song, "You can have life if you want it."[174] Eventually 126,566 copies of *Life* were sold.

God had prepared Otis both spiritually and musically to be a leader in the rapidly expanding music ministry in the 1970s.

Otis grew up in an Ohio parsonage where Christian ministry was both a profession and a lifestyle. The gospel proclaimed in public was lived out at home. His father believed that his pastoral duties began with his family. Otis recalled,

> When I was five years old, my mom was out for the evening. Dad and I were talking at the kitchen table about Christ as our personal Savior. I still remember kneeling at a kitchen chair to accept Christ as my own Savior. Everyone has an opinion about what age is right, but five years was right for me. Some months after that we had a baptismal service. Our little church didn't have a baptistery like churches nowadays do, so we went to the river. A good number from our congregation were at the river when I was baptized. That was a significant beginning for me.[175]

The congregations his father served encouraged Otis to grow in his faith. He remembers seeking spiritual renewal during revival meetings and having the congregation surround him as he knelt at the altar. Those supportive relationships encouraged him to totally consecrate himself to God.

Otis also remembers the impact the annual camp meetings had on him. Being with 5,000 Christians from other churches for two weeks of fellowship—both spiritual and social—deeply impressed him. "There were so many people who were greatly committed to the Lord. I was young, and there were times when I would chuckle a little bit about the actions of some people, and yet it was making an impression on me. There were those who would get blessed and shout and raise their hands and put their hankies in the air. But I think the environment of camp meeting and my church really made an impact on my life. I'll never forget those days."[176]

Love thro' Christ has brought us together, Melting our hearts as one. By God's Spirit we are united, One thro' His blessed Son.

We are one in the bond of love; We are one in the bond of love. We have joined our spirits with the Spirit of God; We are one in the bond of love.*

The camp meetings expanded his musical horizons as well. Otis was amazed that the pianist could play so many notes at once. And his eyes opened wide with delight as the song leader urged the congregation to exuberant praise with his trombone pointed heavenward.

Otis's parents were musical, but not trained. His father sometimes sang bass in a men's quartet. His mother didn't read music but played the piano. "She could play quite well in the key of B♭," Otis recalls with delight. During his junior high days the family often attended local gospel sings.

The formal development of his own musical skill started in the fourth grade when the music teacher taught the class to play the Tonette. Every year all the elementary schools in town would join to form a mass Tonette choir. In the sixth grade he started playing the trombone in the school band. These simple beginnings laid a good foundation for future musical growth.

Otis had played the piano for as long as he can remember, even playing in church services, but he had not enrolled in formal study until he took piano lessons in the seventh grade. He studied for a year. No one at that time could foresee his future ministry as a piano soloist and recording artist.

His spiritual interest and musical talent were bonded through involvement in Youth for Christ.

When I was a junior in high school the director of Youth for Christ in Dayton (Ohio), Ivan Sisk, called me. I had never heard of him. I had never heard of Youth for Christ. Ivan said, "We're having a talent contest, and I heard that you play the piano. Would you be interested in entering the contest?" I said, "Sure, I'd be happy to." He asked me what I might want to play and I said, "Well, why don't I play 'The Holy City.'" A month after that I went to Youth for Christ for the first time. My eyes just bugged out. It was such a new experience. One thousand teenagers. Ivan was a fine preacher with lots of flair and humor and the things that young people enjoyed. It was so alive with energy. It just really caught my attention. Without a doubt, those Youth for Christ experiences expanded my mind and prepared my heart for a bigger ministry to come.[177]

Otis became involved with Youth for Christ at various levels. After he graduated from high school, he studied at the St. Paul Bible College, then returned to Dayton as a Youth for Christ staff member. A year later he moved to San Diego where he served with Youth for Christ for nine years.

As Otis looks back on many years of music ministry—composing and arranging, performing as a soloist, directing church choirs—he is grateful that God has chosen to use him to build the kingdom of God. He said:

I am thankful that the Lord can take any ability that I might have and use it in a much greater way. Maybe I could have made it in show business. Who knows? I'm glad I didn't go that way. Maybe I could have become a classical orchestra conductor. I possibly could have done that OK. But I think that the involvement I've been able to have in the Christian ministry of music has been a significant one. Without a doubt, there will be many people in heaven because of music ministry. I think it's a great responsibility and opportunity.[178]

"Lord, We Praise You" (*Sing to the Lord* No. 135)

While composers often want to be remembered for their most intricate works, the most sung songs by Otis Skillings are his simple choruses. "Lord, We Praise You" was first published as part of the musical *Celebration of Hope*. A proverbial statement that Otis adopted as a guiding principle is that "church hasn't started 'til the people start to sing." In most of his musicals he included simple songs that the congregation could learn quickly and thus actively participate in the service.

"The Bond of Love" (*Sing to the Lord* No. 682)

"The Bond of Love" was written for the musical *Love* in 1971. The refrain has been used in church services and evangelistic crusades around the world. Recently Otis was on a mission trip to the Philippines where a crowd of Bible college students and pastors met him at the airport. As he entered the terminal he saw signs that read "The Bond of Love." When he approached the group they started to sing "We are one in the bond of love," first in English, then in Tagalog, and a third time in Cebuano. In that moment Otis and his new friends experienced the biblical truth he had expressed in a song 25 years earlier.

Gloria Gaither
(1942-)

On September 27, 1981, Gloria Gaither awoke at a truck stop in west Texas as the Gaither Trio traveled through southern states on their fall tour. This morning Gloria met "one well-traded woman who seemed to have not been a person for a long time."[179] The woman's pain-etched face overshadowed Gloria's memory of hundreds of joyful expressions she'd seen at the previous evening's concert.

The truck stop woman had been misused, and after spending three years with her current "love," had been abandoned at the truck stop. Gloria listened to the woman but felt her assistance was inadequate. Gloria returned to the tour bus haunted by the woman's plight and frustrated by her own seemingly meager efforts to show Christ's love.

Gloria Gaither and her husband/collaborator, Bill, believe that living the Christian life is more important than writing or talking or singing about it. They assert that only as they live the gospel can they communicate it clearly.

I then shall live as one
who's learned compassion;
I've been so loved
that I'll risk loving too.
I know how fear
builds walls instead of bridges;
I dare to see
another's point of view.
And when relationships
demand commitment,
Then I'll be there
to care and follow through.*

For example, as their careers in gospel music shifted into high gear in the 1970s, the Gaithers were torn between their parental responsibilities and ministry demands. The children won. Gloria said, "We don't want to be in the spot where we're telling people to be with their kids—work with them, and play with them—and then not be

---

**© Copyright 1981 by Gaither Music Company. All rights reserved. Used by permission.

with ours."[180] So they started accepting concert invitations only for weekends so they could spend each week at home with their children. In doing so they lived the principles they found in Scripture.

Gloria grew up in a Michigan parsonage where the basic tenets of Christianity were applied to everyday living. Of her parents Gloria wrote, "Pastoring was never a thing apart from what they were at home, nor a demand that took them from us. It was instead a calling that all of us shared, something we did together."[181]

Gloria's family worshiped together each evening. Her father would read a scripture passage and the family would discuss it. Then each family member would pray. One summer evening in 1946, Gloria "felt a growing gap between what I was on the inside and what I tried to pretend on the outside."[182] That day had been especially difficult for the four-year-old, and a sense of guilt overwhelmed her.

> I can still see the scene in the living room that night with the whole family kneeling in prayer. Finally, I couldn't fight back the tears anymore. I crawled across to where my mother was kneeling and whispered, "I have to pray." . . . She understood immediately what I meant and stopped my dad in the middle of his sentence. He and my sister came to where I was and put their arms around me as I began to sob out my need for forgiveness. Like the child I was, I simply confessed everything I could think of that stood between me and a clear relationship with them and God and asked Jesus to take control of my life and make me new again. He did. The heaviness of guilt I had felt lifted, and I knew I could soar again. I was a child again, all clean and new. I had been "born" again.[183]

As an adult Gloria discovered that the forgiveness she experienced as a child was just the beginning of her spiritual life. She wrote, "I wanted more than anything to do always those things that are good and right in God's sight. But the list was so long and there were sublists to worry about—feeling proud that I was so truthful [or] analyzing my real motives for being so generous."[184] She described her internal conflict as a "gray feeling that somewhere, somehow, I had missed the mark."[185]

Gloria had heard other people talk about "letting go," "surrendering all," "total commitment," the "second blessing," the "infilling." She made many trips to the altar seeking sanctification. But the struggle continued. Until one day she simply gave up.

> Finally, weary and exhausted and sick of trying, I said something like, "I've had it!" I don't even know if it was a *bona*

fide prayer or just a cry from the depths of my being. But the cry went something like this: "I'm sick of trying. I'm going to quit trying! I'm exhausted in my heart. I don't want to go back, but work as I may I can't get ahead. I'm giving up. It's up to You. If You can't keep me, I'm finished with the struggle!" There wasn't a flash of lightning or a voice from heaven. I didn't begin to speak in another language. There was only a quiet— somewhere in the very depths of my being.[186]

Gloria began to understand her spiritual turmoil as a battle of whether or not she would let Jesus be Lord of her life. She wrote, "I have learned that it is one thing to accept Jesus as Savior and Redeemer and have our sins forgiven, and it is quite another thing to let Jesus come into our lives as Lord."[187]

Gloria Gaither expresses her spiritual and life experiences in her songs. In regard to songwriting Bill Gaither wrote, "I have to experience [the] intangible to be able to express it musically, and, if I theorize without tasting, my creative juices dry up."[188] He added, "I have never written for commercial success. I just wrote what was in my heart and in my gut."[189] The honesty and practicality of the Gaithers' songs have resonated in the hearts of people around the world. Their songs express the life of faith, a faith that works.

All my tomorrows, all my past,
Jesus is Lord of all.
I've quit my struggles,
contentment at last!
Jesus is Lord of all.*

"Because He Lives" (*Sing to the Lord* No. 256)

A confluence of personal and societal traumas influenced the creation of "Because He Lives."

A close, non-Christian friend questioned the Gaithers' motives, accusing them of being in music ministry only for financial gain. Bill and Gloria checked their relationships with the Lord and God assured them that everything was OK. But the antagonist continued. Bill wrote, "Then at a huge gathering my accuser cornered me and leveled the charges personally. . . . 'You're a phony,' he said, 'and you know it.' 'That's not true,' was all I could manage."[190]

During this time, Bill was ill with mononucleosis. The combination of physical illness and vicious attack sent him "into a black hole"[191] of depression. Some days he did little more than lie on his back and cry.

Meanwhile, Gloria was pregnant with their third child. On New Year's Eve she sat alone in her living room thinking about recent events in the United States. The social upheaval of the 1960s deposited drug use and violence and anti-Christian thought throughout the country. Gloria wondered, "Who in their right mind would bring a child into a world like this? The world is so evil. Influences beyond our control are so strong. What will happen to this child?"[192]

Both Bill and Gloria began to see the risen Lord as the answer to their questions, and after their son, Benjy, was born, they wrote:

> How sweet to hold a newborn baby
> And feel the pride and joy he gives;
> But greater still the calm assurance:
> This child can face uncertain days because He lives.*

Although those lines were written first, they became stanza 2 of the song. From that beginning they crafted the song that people of God love to sing.

"Something Beautiful" (*Sing to the Lord* No. 355)

Bill Gaither wrote:

> One Monday morning, after a wonderful weekend of singing and seeing people respond to "Because He Lives," Gloria and I were marveling over God's goodness. We looked at our three precious children and thought of the experience of sharing that song with appreciative people and how that had warmed our hearts. "You know what?" I said, "Despite all this stuff we've been going through, God has still done something beautiful in our lives." It doesn't take much to get Gloria started thinking and writing. Not long after that she came to me with a poem that would become the lyric for "Something Beautiful."[193]

"The Family of God" (*Sing to the Lord* No. 681)

On the Saturday before Easter in 1970, a man from the Gaithers' church was injured in an explosion. Ron Garner was working as a mechanic in a garage when a blast blew the building apart and started a fire. Ron was burned severely. As emergency personnel hurried him to the hospital, people from the church quickly called others to pray. The doctors offered little hope, but Christians kept praying.

"On Easter morning a weary congregation gathered for worship. Nobody felt much like celebrating. . . . About twenty minutes into the service, the pastor came in with a report from the hospital. Although he had gone without sleep to be with the Garner family through the long hours, there was sunshine in his eyes. 'Ron has outlived the deadline. The doctors say he has a chance. They are going to begin treatment.' . . . New life was infused into us all."[194]

On the way home from church, the Gaithers talked about the congregation's response to the Garner family's needs. They were moved by how people pledged to help the Garners: child care, transportation to the hospital, donated blood, money, meals. When they arrived home Gloria started preparing dinner while Bill played the piano. Gloria wrote, "It wasn't long before the magnetism of the chorus Bill was singing drew me from the kitchen to the piano."[195] When they completed the song, the family sat down to Easter dinner.

OTHER HYMNS BY GLORIA GAITHER

"There's Something About That Name" (*Sing to the Lord* No. 148)
"Jesus Is Lord of All" (*Sing to the Lord* No. 275)
"Come, Holy Spirit" (*Sing to the Lord* No. 308)
"I Will Serve Thee" (*Sing to the Lord* No. 469)
"Gentle Shepherd" (*Sing to the Lord* No. 626)
"I Then Shall Live" (*Sing to the Lord* No. 732)

FOR FURTHER READING

Gaither, Bill. *I Almost Missed the Sunset.* Nashville: Thomas Nelson Publishers, 1992.
Gaither, Gloria. *Because He Lives.* Old Tappan, N.J.: Fleming H. Revell Company, 1977.
———. *Fully Alive!* Nashville: Thomas Nelson Publishers, 1984.
———. *We Have This Moment.* Waco, Tex.: Word Books, 1988.
Walton, Samuel B. "People Like Honest Sounds." The *Saturday Evening Post* 248 (April 1977): 46-47, 99, 102.

Stephen R. Adams
(1943-)

Steve was only 7 years old when he first thought about writing gospel songs. His piano teacher, Rita Rundlett, was the wife of a Nazarene pastor. When her husband died suddenly she needed to provide for her family. Steve's father, Nathan A. Adams Jr., also a Nazarene pastor, offered his home and his piano one day a week as a studio for Rita to give lessons. Rita came to the Adams home every Wednesday and often stayed for dinner, then attended the prayer meeting. Attempting to deal with her grief, Rita started writing songs and bringing them with her. Steve's father would sing as Rita played. And Steve wondered if someday he might write songs like that.

Steve was only 13 years old when he wrote his first song. He was attending a camp meeting at Portsmouth, Rhode Island, when he found a piano and wrote the song. Steve didn't write many other songs during his teenage years, but his desire to communicate the gospel through music increased.

At 17 Steve was entering his senior year in high school when he completely consecrated his life to God. Steve had been converted several years before and had served as a pianist and singer in his local church, at camp meetings, and at many events on the New England District of the Church of the Nazarene. But one Sunday morning he gave himself *totally* to God.

Steve's parents had moved to Indiana where his father pastored Frankfort First Church of the Nazarene. Steve had received a scholarship to study "The Art of Communication" at the Andover Academy, so he stayed in Massachusetts for the summer in a town where he didn't know anyone. On his second Sunday there, Steve looked for a place to attend a worship service. Walking through town, he saw a church building constructed in the typical New England style of architecture. He entered the place in which God would meet him. Just before the sermon three ladies stood to sing.

> That is the point at which I really feel that there was a supernatural call to songwriting. I had it as a child, but it was

reawakened at this time. The ladies stood and sang out of the hymnal accompanied by a very poor pipe organ. It wasn't played well. It wasn't a great production. It was the lyric of the song that touched my life.

> *O Jesus, I have promised*
> *To serve Thee to the end;*
> *Be Thou forever near me,*
> *My Master and my Friend:*
> *I shall not fear the battle*
> *If Thou art by my side,*
> *Nor wander from the pathway*
> *If Thou wilt be my guide.*

I remember walking out of that service onto the street corner saying "That is my commitment."[196]

At 26, Steve had graduated from Indiana University with a bachelor's degree in philosophy and a master's degree in literature. After graduation he taught English at the junior high school in Lebanon, Indiana. For 2 years Steve taught school Monday through Friday; then Gene Braun, a gospel singer, would pick him up on Friday afternoon for a weekend of concerts. At the end of 2 years Steve knew something had to

> *Thro' disappointment and danger, too,*
> *Thro' labors and sorrows we've come!*
> *But God's grace has guided safely thro',*
> *And it will surely lead us home!*

change or his body would give out. He needed to give himself either to education or to gospel music. "After the kids had gone home one afternoon, I was erasing things from the chalkboard when I felt like the Lord said to me, 'There are some other writings I want you to do that will not be erased.'"[197] And the work for which God had prepared him for 20 years began in earnest.

In his songs Steve looks at life experiences from a faith perspective. Steve said, "The poetry that comes from my soul is a reflection of a personal response to the Lord's involvement in my life."[198]

For example, one day in April 1974 Steve was driving in Xenia, Ohio, where he served as the minister of music, when he saw a funnel cloud headed straight toward him. Knowing he could not outrun and outmaneuver the tornado, he stopped his car and ran into a furniture store, diving under an overturned sofa for protection. Steve lay on the floor of the furniture store as the tornado destroyed the building. After the winds died, Steve spent a long time digging himself out. This experience inspired Steve to write "Peace in the Midst of the Storm."

Steve has often known the trauma of adversity. His father died at age 48 from a massive cardiac arrest. Steve could not work for two-and-a-half years because of a health problem. He knows the tension of financial distress. For five years Steve and his brother, Nate, cared for their mother who suffered with Alzheimer's disease. In every case he learned that God is faithful.

In the Christian life there are hills and valleys, suffering and laughter. Through my ordeals I've learned to trust the resurrected and resurrecting power of Christ. I opened the Bible one night, turned to Eph. 1:19-20 and read, "I pray that you will begin to understand how incredibly great his power is to help those who believe him. It is that same mighty power that raised Christ from the dead" (TLB). I remember reading those verses and thinking, "By faith I'm going to appropriate that truth." God always brings triumph out of tragedy.[199]

"Where the Spirit of the Lord Is" (*Sing to the Lord* No. 310)

Steve wrote "Where the Spirit of the Lord Is" near the end of a service in which the Lord's supernatural presence filled the room. He was presenting concerts and revival services with Gene Braun. One morning God poured out the Holy Spirit while Gene sang. The song was not one usually used as an invitation hymn, but a dozen young couples spontaneously came to the altar to pray. Inspired by God, Steve wrote "Where the Spirit of the Lord Is" while playing another song on the piano during the prayer time. He recalled, "I was sitting at the piano when the Lord dumped that song in my lap. I kept on playing with my left hand and wrote the song with my right hand. It was a moment of extreme blessing in my heart."[200]

"All Because of God's Amazing Grace" (*Sing to the Lord* No. 354)

In the late 1960s and early 1970s Bill Gaither organized a group of gospel singers to present Friday and Saturday night concerts in Midwest high school auditoriums. Occasionally he called Steve to join the team to accompany Doug Oldham. One night at the high school in New Haven, Indiana, Henry and Hazel Slaughter talked with the people about the grace of God. Steve said, "I remember Henry turning to his wife and saying, 'All that we are and all that we can ever hope to be, honey, is all because of God's amazing grace at work in our lives.'"[201]

All weekend that phrase repeated in Steve's mind. Steve thought about his wife, Jan, and his infant son. He recognized that God was the source of everything he treasured. "Henry had vocalized what I thought about life."[202]

The following Monday Steve sat down at the spinet in his house and wrote "All Because of God's Amazing Grace." When he completed it, he called his wife, who was a receptionist in a dental office, and sang the song to her over the phone.

As Steve reflects on his years of music ministry, both as a gospel songwriter and a church musician, he realizes his mission has been to help people come to know the loving God who, in grace, gives gifts to needy people. His message simply affirms that every blessing we receive is "all because of God's amazing grace."

Steve Adams was encouraged by Bill and Gloria Gaither as the scope of his music ministry began to enlarge. For more information on the Gaithers, see pages 98-102.

FOR FURTHER READING

Tracy, Wesley, ed. "Steve Adams: That Which I Treasure and Hold Dear." *Herald of Holiness* 80 (July 1991): 25, 44.

Ken Bible
(1950-)

Ken Bible thought it would only be a short trip as he drove his wife, Gloria, to the home decorating show. But that became the catalyst for a major adjustment in his spiritual journey.

Ken's spiritual growth had brought him to the place where he was frustrated with his ineffectiveness at sharing the good news with unbelievers. Ken had worked at Lillenas Publishing Company for 19 years as music editor and as director. He knew the secular world largely ignored the productions of Christian media, so his efforts through his job missed unbelievers. He also knew that the secular media largely ignored the Christian community, so he had little chance of finding a platform in that setting.

As he walked through the home decorating show, Ken didn't see the displays. Instead, he saw people—elbow to elbow—looking for ways to make their lives more satisfying. His contemplation continued as he drove home. On the left he passed a huge electronics store filled with people looking for entertainment. On the right was a giant sporting goods store with scores of people looking for leisure gear. He drove by a major bookstore, crowded with people looking for intellectual stimulation. Ken realized that these people were looking for something—anything—to make their lives more fulfilled. And he was doing little to share with them the abundant life that Jesus offers.

Then God broke through.

I've never heard God speak audibly. Often when God speaks it is through impressions and a tug on my heart. But there have been a couple of times when it seemed like God was speaking actual words to me. This time it seemed like God was asking, "What could you do if nothing else mattered?" That stopped me short. I didn't know the answer to it.

I had been reading in 1 John 2:6, which says that if we claim to follow Christ we should walk as He walked. So I started a study of the synoptic gospels, asking these questions: How did Christ walk? and, therefore, How should I walk?[203]

In the following days, as Ken pondered this experience, the Lord prepared an opportunity for him to answer the questions with action. His church, the Kansas City First Church of the Nazarene, announced a new effort to reach their neighborhood for Christ. Ken and Gloria signed up. In the first year the outreach program, Neighbor to Neighbor, reached 520 homes with two contacts each month. The second year they moved into another area of 800 homes. Ken wrote two series of monthly flyers, titled "For Your Consideration" and "Living the Natural Way," designed to draw unbelievers to Christ. He was on the front lines seeking the lost, just like Jesus.

Ken's desire to communicate the good news of Jesus Christ is a dominant color in the tapestry of his life. His personal journey of faith started when, as a 10-year-old, he knelt at his mother's bed. Ken's home church provided many opportunities to express his faith. As a freshman in high school, Ken was asked one Sunday morning to preach in the evening service. He doesn't remember how long he spoke, but he's sure the congregation went home earlier than usual. Ken majored in music composition at the University of Cincinnati's Conservatory of Music and wrote a few pieces for the church. But he had not yet found his calling.

Come now, Father, shape our ways.
We will use the light You give,
In Your Spirit serve and grow,
Learn how love would have us live;
*Learn how love would have us live.**

Wanting to know God's Word more fully prompted Ken to teach himself New Testament Greek. He later learned some biblical Hebrew on his own. These self-directed studies increased his thirst for a greater understanding of the things of God. So he applied and was accepted as a student at Nazarene Theological Seminary. During a trip to Kansas City to look for a job, however, Ken was offered a position as the music editor at Lillenas Publishing Company. He accepted the job and never did attend seminary.

Ken's keen interest in Bible study made him a natural choice as a Sunday School teacher. He became "convinced that scriptural truth could be communicated in a way that was deep and thought-provoking, but yet was understandable by the average person in the pew."[204] When he started writing hymns to use in the Bible studies he led, Ken discovered a special ministry. He now knew God's will for his life: to arrange words in meter and rhyme so others might know the Word of Life.

Ken was almost 40 years old when everything seemed to fall into place. He had wanted to write for many years, but family and job responsibilities had taken priority. He now believes that "we seem to underestimate how much preparation the Lord wants to put us through to do a job. We always think that we're ready before God thinks that we're ready."[205] Ken believes that God's timing in his life was perfect.

The main lesson Ken needed to learn was to trust God completely, every moment of every day.

I wanted all that God had for me, but I didn't know quite how to get it. I tried self-discipline. By basic nature that's kind of me anyway. I tried study because I thought that there might be some deep, hidden secrets that I could learn by study. And what I found out is that the essence of the gospel is not dug out by self-discipline and it is not some hidden secret known only to the wisest among us, but it is living out the very simple truth that all God really expects for us in all of Scripture is simply to trust Him in a meaningful and heartfelt way. There is no one-time experience that makes the day-by-day decisions unnecessary. We still have to follow God one step at a time in simple trust. That realization changed my outlook.[206]

As Ken's journey with Jesus became more intimate, he discovered that his hymn texts became more compelling. As he wrote from his heart—knowing experientially the truth he expressed—the testimony he sought to share rang out with clarity. The course of his life has been set: "to communicate the truth of the Scripture in penetrating and practical terms."[207]

"Adoration" (*Sing to the Lord* No. 203)

In the late 1970s Ken began collecting hymns—both old and new. He realized that Lillenas Publishing Company would one day publish another hymnal. His hymn collection became the main resource for the *Sing to the Lord* hymnal, and Ken received the opportunity to serve as its editor.

Sometimes as he evaluated an old hymn he would envision a new choral setting of the text. Such was the creation of "Adoration." Ken found a hymn text by John S. B. Monsell, which he sent to Tom Fettke to consider using in a choral piece. They decided that the text could be strengthened with a new second stanza that Ken wrote.

Then Tom composed a new tune and the song was first published in an a cappella choral arrangement. "Adoration" has since appeared in four major hymnals.

"Raised from Death to Love and Living" (*Sing to the Lord* No. 511)

In March 1983 Ken was leading the Wednesday evening Bible study at the Grandview, Missouri, Church of the Nazarene. As he prepared for the study of 1 Pet. 1:14-21, Ken found a description of how Christians are to live. God is holy and calls us to be holy. God cares for us like a father, and we are to trust Him. God is the Righteous Judge, and we are to be watchful. The outline of the Bible study Ken prepared became the outline for "Raised from Death to Love and Living." It was first sung at the close of that Wednesday evening service in March 1983 as the summary of the Bible study.

"Father, Speak Your Word Again" (*Sing to the Lord* No. 690)

Ken wrote "Father, Speak Your Word Again" for the Wednesday evening Bible study group he led in 1983. The original inscription read "A prayer before Bible study." The group sang it at the beginning of each session for several weeks.

Like "Raised from Death to Love and Living" and "Father, Speak Your Word Again," Ken wrote other hymns for the Wednesday evening Bible study group. He always utilized a familiar hymn tune and usually used the new hymn as the summary for the Bible study.

Epilogue

For more than two years I have been involved with researching and writing this book. At first I had a broad idea of what I wanted to do—record the hymn stories and spiritual biographies of Wesleyan/Holiness hymn writers. As I gathered materials, my focus moved from wide-angle to telescopic as I examined the lives and ministries of specific individuals. In the last few days, as I have written the final chapters, I have stepped back for another wide-angle perspective. When compared with my first impressions, the panorama now has much more definition.

In reflection I have noted that some writers' experiences were similar to those of another. Trends began to emerge. Granted, the hymn writers profiled in this book were not selected in a highly scientific, random fashion. The persons included here were ones for whom I found adequate resources to tell both their spiritual journeys *and* how their songs were written. I have reams of paper on other hymn writers within the Wesleyan/Holiness Movement for whom I have testimonies or hymn stories, but not both. In spite of this disclaimer on the limitations of my sample, several common elements seem significant.

I'm impressed with the number of hymn writers who testified to pivotal spiritual experiences while they were children or teenagers. Mary James, Byron Carmony, Otis Skillings, Gloria Gaither, and Ken Bible were converted as children. Almost all of the writers discussed in this book were raised in Christian families. Some grew up in parsonages. When they were young these hymn writers were thoroughly taught about God. As a result of their testimonies, I'm challenged to be a better father and to provide good spiritual care for the children in my church.

Another important element common to the hymn writers is that their most life-transforming spiritual experiences were crisis events. Most were born into Christian families; all of them were born again into the family of God at a moment in time. Recognizing this, I have strengthened my resolve to work evangelistically as God leads.

As I prepared this book I noticed the number of people who were active in the church while they were still children and teenagers. Otis Skillings was a church pianist as a child. Mary James taught Sunday School at age 12. Byron Carmony was the Sunday School superintendent when he was 17. George Beverly Shea started singing solos as a teenager. Barney Warren joined an evangelistic team before he turned 20.

In our interview, Otis Skillings talked about the benefit of growing up in small churches where he had many opportunities for involvement. That was my experience as well. My two brothers, sister, and I grew up in a parsonage. Our father, Rev. LeRoy C. Schwanz, served small- to intermediate-sized congregations in Nebraska and Oregon for more than 30 years. Now two of us are pastors, one is a missionary, and the other is a minister of music. We've talked about the on-the-job ministerial training we received while we were still young. Paul urged Timothy to not "let anyone look down on you because you are young, but set an example for the believers in speech, in life, in love, in faith and in purity" (1 Tim. 4:12). In response to this observation I'm committed to finding ways to increase children's participation in my church.

As I reread the chapters of this book, I realized that these people were involved in many forms of Christian service. They did not put themselves in a hymn-writer-only box or a church-musician-only box. Phoebe Palmer led Bible studies. Mary James taught Sunday School. Fanny Crosby worked in city missions. Henry Gilmour and Lelia Morris were camp meeting workers. Charles Jones founded a Holiness denomination. Barney Warren, Haldor Lillenas, and Byron Carmony were pastors. Lorene Good was a missionary, and Otis Skillings is involved in a ministry of encouraging missionaries. In an age of specialization, I'm challenged to constantly add tools to my ministry toolbox. I'm not just a church musician. I'm not just a writer. Instead, I'm a servant of the Lord, presenting myself to God for service without conditions.

One other observation. About half of the hymn writers included in this book suffered severe infirmities. Fanny Crosby and Lelia Morris were blind. Annie Johnson Flint was paralyzed with arthritis. Clara Tear Williams and Lorene Good endured tuberculosis. Thomas Chisholm had a complete breakdown that forced him out of pastoral ministry. Steve Adams faced severe vocal problems for several years. God miraculously healed some. Others were testimonies that God's grace is sufficient. But in all cases it seems God used the infirmity to focus divine power, like a magnifying glass and sunlight on a summer day. In response I've decided to complain less and to look expectantly for God to create good out of difficult situations.

The writer of Heb. 11 narrates a tour of the faith hall of fame. The next chapter admonishes those still in the race to find courage and strength in the examples of those who have crossed the finish line. As I have lived with these hymn writers during the past two years, my resolve to be a faithful disciple has intensified. I hope their stories have also deepened your faith and strengthened your spiritual quest.

Now to him who is able to do immeasurably more than all we ask or imagine, according to his power that is at work within us, to him be glory in the church and in Christ Jesus throughout all generations, for ever and ever! Amen *(Eph. 3:20-21).*

Notes

1. Edmund S. Lorenz, *Church Music* (New York: Fleming H. Revell, 1923), 335.

2. S. Olin Garrison, *Forty Witnesses* (New York: Eaton and Mains, 1888), 253.

3. Charles Edward White, *The Beauty of Holiness* (Grand Rapids: Francis Asbury Press, 1986), 7.

4. Ibid., 8.

5. Garrison, *Forty Witnesses*, 253.

6. Ibid., 254.

7. Ibid., 255.

8. Ibid., 257-58.

9. Carl Bangs, *Phineas F. Bresee: His Life in Methodism, the Holiness Movement, and the Church of the Nazarene* (Kansas City: Beacon Hill Press of Kansas City, 1995), 222.

10. White, *The Beauty of Holiness*, 27.

11. George Hughes, *Days of Power in the Forest Temple* (Boston: John Bent, 1873), 253.

12. Joseph H. James, *The Life of Mrs. Mary D. James* (New York: Palmer and Hughes, 1886), 39.

13. Ibid., 5.

14. Ibid.

15. Ibid., 16.

16. Ibid., 97.

17. Ibid., 97-98.

18. Ibid., 240.

19. Ibid., 3.

20. Ibid., 199.

21. E. A. Girvin, *Phineas F. Bresee: A Prince in Israel* (Kansas City: Nazarene Publishing House, 1916), 366.

22. Robert Lowry, "Biographical Sketch," in *Bells at Evening and Other Verses*, 5th ed., Fanny J. Crosby (New York: Biglow and Main Company, 1903), 11.

23. Ibid., 14.

24. Fanny J. Crosby, *Memories of Eighty Years* (Boston: James H. Earle, 1906), 96.

25. Fanny J. Crosby, *Fanny Crosby's Life-Story* (New York: Everywhere Publishing Company, 1903), 114.

26. Lorenz, *Church Music*, 334.

27. George C. Stebbins, *Reminiscences and Gospel Hymn Stories* (New York: George H. Doran Company, 1924), 278.

28. Bernard Ruffin, *Fanny Crosby* (Philadelphia: United Church Press, 1976), 153.

29. Crosby, *Eighty Years*, 171.

30. Ibid., 166.

31. Lowry, "Autobiographical Sketch," 21-22.

32. March 24, 1908. Quoted in Ruffin, *Fanny Crosby,* 136.

33. Crosby, *Eighty Years*, 152-53.

34. Ibid., 144.

35. Cliff Barrows, ed., *Crusade Hymn Stories* (Chicago: Hope Publishing Co., 1967), 93.

36. See Crosby, *Eighty Years,* 170, 189; Crosby, *Life-Story,* 117; Lowry, "Autobiographical Sketch," 14-15; and Ruffin, *Fanny Crosby,* 105.

37. Crosby, *Eighty Years,* 138.

38. Ibid.

39. Fred A. Mund, *Keep the Music Ringing* (Kansas City: Nazarene Publishing House, 1979), 11.

40. Stebbins, *Memoirs and Reminiscences,* 105-6.

41. William J. Reynolds, *Songs of Glory* (Grand Rapids: Zondervan, 1990), 226.

42. Crosby, *Eighty Years,* 168.

43. Ibid., 176-77.

44. Crosby, *Life-Story,* 128-29.

45. Lowry, "Autobiographical Sketch," 17.

46. Crosby, *Eighty Years,* 178.

47. Reynolds, *Songs of Glory,* 256.

48. Ruffin, *Fanny Crosby,* 28.

49. Kenneth W. Osbeck, *101 Hymn Stories* (Grand Rapids: Kregel Publications, 1982), 167.

50. Crosby, *Eighty Years,* 144-45.

51. [Mrs. E. E. Williams] *An Account of Pentecostal Services on the Allegheny Mountains at Mountain Lake Park, Garrett Co., Maryland, Which Commenced Saturday Morning July 7th, and Closed Monday Night, July 16th, 1894* (Philadelphia: John Thompson, 1894), 7-23.

52. A. J. Showalter, *The Best Gospel Songs and Their Composers* (Dalton, Ga.: A. J. Showalter Company, 1904), n.p.

53. William J. Reynolds, *Companion to Baptist Hymnal (1975)* (Nashville: Broadman Press, 1976), 319.

54. [Williams] *Pentecostal Services . . . 1894,* 183-84.

55. Ibid., 173.

56. Ibid., 184-85.

57. Ibid., 185.

58. Ibid.

59. Ibid., 41.

60. Ibid., 133.

61. [Mrs. E. E. Williams] *An Account of Pentecostal Services on the Allegheny Mountains at Mountain Lake Park, Garrett Co., Maryland, Which Commenced Saturday Morning July 3rd, and Closed Monday Night, July 12th, 1897* (Philadelphia: Christian Standard Company, 1897), 3.

62. Ibid., 88.

63. Harold La Penna, *Hymn Search: The Hymnists and the Hymns of Ocean Grove* (Ocean Grove, N.J.: Self-published, 1994), 3.

64. Reynolds, *Companion to Baptist Hymnal,* 384.

65. Haldor Lillenas, *Modern Gospel Song Stories* (Kansas City: Lillenas Publishing Company, 1952), 17.

66. S. B. Shaw, ed., *Echoes of the General Holiness Convention Held in Chicago May 3-13, 1901* (Chicago: S. B. Shaw, Publisher, 1901), 179.

67. Clara Tear Williams, "Life of Clara Tear Williams" (Houghton, N.Y.: Houghton College, Willard J. Houghton Library).

68. Ibid.

69. Ibid.

70. Ibid.

71. Ibid.

72. Ibid.

73. Ibid.

74. Barrows, ed., *Crusade Hymn Stories*, 75.

75. Williams, "The Life of Clara Tear Williams."

76. George W. Sanville, *Forty Gospel Hymn Stories* (Winona Lake, Ind.: Rodeheaver-Hall Mack Company, 1943), 28.

77. Mary Ethel Wiess, *Singing at Her Work: A Biography of Mrs. C. H. Morris* (Kansas City: Nazarene Publishing House, 1934, 1953), 32.

78. Ibid., 13.

79. Ibid., 7.

80. Ibid., 12.

81. Ibid.

82. Ibid., 30.

83. Ibid., 33.

84. Charles H. Gabriel, *The Singers and Their Songs* (Winona Lake, Ind.: Rodeheaver Company, 1915), 19.

85. Wiess, *Singing at Her Work*, 33-34.

86. Charles Price Jones, "Autobiographical Sketch of Charles Price Jones Founder of the Church of Christ (Holiness) U.S.A.," *The Journal of Black Sacred Music* 2 (Fall 1988): 52.

87. Ibid., "The History of My Songs," 63.

88. Ibid.

89. Ibid., 73.

90. Ibid., "Autobiographical Sketch," 53.

91. Ibid.

92. Ibid., 54.

93. Ibid., 55.

94. Ibid., 54-55.

95. Ibid., "History," 74.

96. Ibid., 63.

97. Ibid.

98. Ibid., 64.

99. Ibid., 63.

100. T. O. Chisholm to David Livingstone Ives, April 17, 1949.

101. Suzanna Clark, "Songs of an Unsung Servant," *Hymn Lovers' Magazine* 5 (July/August 1951): 37.

102. Ibid.

103. Gabriel, *The Singers and Their Songs*, 76.

104. Kenneth W. Osbeck, *101 More Hymn Stories* (Grand Rapids: Kregel Publications, 1985), 178.

105. Osbeck, *101 Hymn Stories*, 84.

106. James Draper, *More than a Song: Little Known Stories About 30 Favorite Gospel Songs and Hymns* (Chicago: Moody Press, 1970), 40.

107. Ovella Satre Shafer, "David Livingstone Ives," *Conquest* 11 (December 1956): 44.

108. Clark, "Songs of an Unsung Servant," 14.

109. Phil Kerr, *Music in Evangelism and Stories of Famous Christian Songs* (Glendale, Calif.: Gospel Music Publishers, 1939), 145.

110. Clark, "Songs of an Unsung Servant," 14-15.

111. Rowland Victor Bingham, *The Life of Annie Johnson Flint* (Grand Rapids: Zondervan Publishing House, n.d.), 20.

112. Ibid.

113. Ibid., 53-54.

114. Annie Johnson Flint, *Annie Johnson Flint's Best Loved Poems* (Toronto: Evangelical Publishers, 1955), 59.

115. Ibid., 7.

116. Bingham, *The Life of Annie Johnson Flint*, 38-39.

117. Flint, *Best Loved Poems*, 87.

118. Ibid., 45.

119. Lawrence R. Schoenhals, *Companion to Hymns of Faith and Life* (Winona Lake, Ind.: Light and Life Press, 1980), 276-77.

120. Andrew L. Byers, *Birth of a Reformation* (Los Angeles: Gospel Trumpet Company, 1921), 337.

121. Ibid., 396.

122. Axchie A. Bolitho, *To the Chief Singer: A Brief Story of the Work and Influence of Barney E. Warren* (Anderson, Ind.: Gospel Trumpet Company, 1942), 26-27.

123. Ibid., 64-65.

124. Ibid., 174.

125. Barney Warren, "Song Stories," *Gospel Trumpet* (February 18, 1939), 10.

126. Martha Lorene Hansen Good, "Sketches of the Past" (unpublished autobiography, n.d.).

127. Deets Pacific Bible College became Pasadena College, then Point Loma Nazarene College.

128. Haldor Lillenas, *Down Melody Lane* (Kansas City: Lillenas Publishing Company, 1953), 23-24.

129. Haldor Lillenas, *Modern Gospel Song Stories* (Kansas City: Lillenas Publishing Company, 1952), 67.

130. Lillenas, *Down Melody Lane*, 13.

131. Ibid., 14-15.

132. Ibid., 19.

133. Stephen S. White, ed., "Dr. Haldor Lillenas," *Herald of Holiness* 48 (September 30, 1959), 15.

134. Lillenas, *Modern Gospel Song Stories*, 105.

135. Ibid., 47.

136. Lillenas, *Down Melody Lane*, 33.

137. Lillenas, *Modern Gospel Song Stories*, 81.

138. Lillenas, *Down Melody Lane*, 34.

139. White, "Dr. Haldor Lillenas," 14.

140. Lillenas, *Modern Gospel Song Stories*, 79.

141. White, "Dr. Haldor Lillenas," 14.

142. Lillenas, *Modern Gospel Song Stories*, 43.

143. Ibid.

144. Lillenas, *Down Melody Lane*, 25.

145. Floyd W. Hawkins, *The Way of Gladness* (Self-published, 1996), 89-90.

146. Ibid., 26.

147. Ibid., 30.

148. Floyd Hawkins, interview by author, September 7, 1996.

149. Hawkins, *The Way of Gladness*, 96.

150. George Beverly Shea and Fred Bauer, *Songs That Lift the Heart* (Old Tappan, N.J.: F. H. Revell, 1972), 14-15.

151. Ibid., 21.

152. Ibid.

153. George Beverly Shea and Fred Bauer, *Then Sings My Soul* (Old Tappan, N.J.: F. H. Revell, 1968), 35-36.

154. Ibid., 36-37.

155. Howard Miller became a general superintendent of the Church of the Nazarene (1940-48). For several years Rhea Miller was a member of the General Council of the Nazarene Foreign Missionary Society.

156. Shea, *Then Sings My Soul*, 47-48.

157. Shea, *Songs That Lift the Heart*, 54.

158. Byron Carmony, interview by author, April 11, 1996.

159. Byron Carmony to author, March 26, 1996.

160. Carmony, interview, April 11, 1996.

161. Ibid.

162. Ibid.

163. Ibid.

164. Ibid.

165. Ibid.

166. Carmony, letter, March 26, 1996.

167. Ibid.

168. Carmony, interview, April 11, 1996.

169. R. Wingrove Ives to Paul William Thomas, October 31, 1973, International Center of The Wesleyan Church, Archives and Historical Library, Indianapolis.

170. R. Wingrove Ives, *A Missionary's Cry from the Island of Barbados* (Kingswood, Ky.: Missionary Office of the Pilgrim Holiness Church [1929]), 15-16.

171. Catherine Ives Fehr to author, April 15, 1996.

172. Richard Gerig to author, January 18, 1996.

173. Otis Skillings, interview by author, April 13, 1996.

174. Ibid.

175. Ibid.

176. Ibid.

177. Ibid.

178. Ibid.

179. Gloria Gaither, *We Have This Moment* (Waco, Tex.: Word Books, 1988), 85.

180. Samuel B. Walton, "People Like Honest Sounds," the *Saturday Evening Post* 248 (April 1977): 99.

181. Gloria Gaither, *Fully Alive!* (Nashville: Thomas Nelson Publishers, 1984), 21-22.

182. Ibid., 22.

183. Ibid., 24.

184. Gloria Gaither, *Because He Lives* (Old Tappan, N.J.: Fleming H. Revell Company, 1977), 81.

185. Ibid., 82.

186. Ibid., 83.

187. Ibid., 85.

188. Bill Gaither, *I Almost Missed the Sunset* (Nashville: Thomas Nelson Publishers, 1992), 7.

189. Ibid., 59.

190. Gaither, *I Almost Missed the Sunset*, 78.

191. Ibid., 79.

192. Gaither, *Because He Lives*, 173-74.

193. Gaither, *I Almost Missed the Sunset*, 87-88.

194. Gaither, *Because He Lives*, 124.

195. Ibid., 125.

196. Steve Adams, interview by author, September 26, 1996.

197. Ibid.

198. Ibid.

199. Ibid.
200. Ibid.
201. Ibid.
202. Ibid.
203. Ken Bible, interview by author, September 20, 1996.
204. Ibid.
205. Ibid.
206. Ibid.
207. Ibid.

Bibliography

Avery, Gordon. *Companion to the Song Book of the Salvation Army.* 4th ed. London: Salvationist Publishing and Supplies, 1970.

Barrows, Cliff, ed. *Crusade Hymn Stories.* Chicago: Hope Publishing Co., 1967.

Buehler, Kathleen D. *Heavenly Song: Stories of Church of God Song Writers and Their Songs.* Anderson, Ind.: Warner Press, 1993.

Claghorn, Gene. *Women Composers and Hymnists.* Metuchen, N.J.: Scarecrow Press, 1984.

Draper, James. *More than a Song: Little Known Stories About 30 Favorite Gospel Songs and Hymns.* Chicago: Moody Press, 1970.

Emurian, Ernest K. *Forty True Stories of Famous Gospel Songs.* Natick, Mass.: W. A. Wilde Co., 1959.

———. *Great Hymns of Testimony.* Nashville: Convention Press, 1976.

———. *Living Stories of Famous Hymns.* Grand Rapids: Baker Book House, 1955.

Gabriel, Charles H. *The Singers and Their Songs.* Winona Lake, Ind.: The Rodeheaver Company, 1915.

Gariepy, Henry. *Songs in the Night.* Grand Rapids: William B. Eerdmans Publishing Company, 1996.

Hall, J. H. *Biography of Gospel Song and Hymn Writers.* New York: Revell, 1914.

Hustad, Donald P. *Dictionary-Handbook to Hymns for the Living Church.* Carol Stream, Ill.: Hope Publishing Company, 1978.

Kerr, Phil. *Music in Evangelism and Stories of Famous Christian Songs.* Glendale, Calif.: Gospel Music Publishers, 1939.

Konkel, Wilbur. *Hymn Stories.* Salem, Ohio: Schmul Publishing Company, 1986.

Lillenas, Haldor. *Modern Gospel Song Stories.* Kansas City: Lillenas Publishing Company, 1952.

Metcalf, Frank J. *American Writers and Compilers of Sacred Music.* New York: Abingdon, 1925.

Osbeck, Kenneth W. *Amazing Grace.* Grand Rapids: Kregel Publications, 1990.

———. *101 Hymn Stories.* Grand Rapids: Kregel Publications, 1982.

———. *101 More Hymn Stories.* Grand Rapids: Kregel Publications, 1985.

Reynolds, William J. *Companion to Baptist Hymnal (1975).* Nashville: Broadman Press, 1976.

———. *Songs of Glory.* Grand Rapids: Zondervan, 1990.

Rodeheaver, Homer A. *Hymnal Handbook for Standard Hymns and Gospel Songs.* Winona Lake, Ind.: Rodeheaver Co., 1931.

Sankey, Ira D. *My Life and the Story of the Gospel Hymns.* New York: Harper and Brothers Publishers, 1906.

Sanville, George W. *Forty Gospel Hymn Stories.* Winona Lake, Ind.: Rodeheaver-Hall Mack Company, 1943.

Schoenhals, Lawrence R. *Companion to Hymns of Faith and Life.* Winona Lake, Ind.: Light and Life Press, 1980.

Showalter, A. J. *The Best Gospel Songs and Their Composers.* Dalton, Ga.: A. J. Showalter Company, 1904.

Stebbins, George C. *Reminiscences and Gospel Hymn Stories.* New York: George H. Doran Company, 1924.

Terry, Lindsay L. *Stories Behind Popular Songs and Hymns.* Grand Rapids: Baker Book House, 1990.

Index of Names

Index of Hymns

(Sing to the Lord hymn numbers in parentheses.)